Liberation
&Human
Wholeness

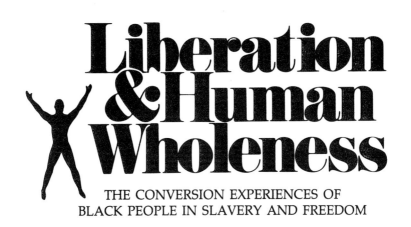

Liberation & Human Wholeness

THE CONVERSION EXPERIENCES OF BLACK PEOPLE IN SLAVERY AND FREEDOM

Edward P. Wimberly
and
Anne Streaty Wimberly

ABINGDON PRESS

NASHVILLE

LIBERATION AND HUMAN WHOLENESS
The Conversion Experiences of Black People in Slavery and Freedom

Library of Congress Cataloging in Publication Data

WIMBERLY, EDWARD P., 1943–
Liberation and human wholeness.

Bibliography: p.
Includes index.
1. Afro-Americans—Religion.   2. Conversion.
3.United States—Church history. I. Wimberly, Anne
Streaty, 1936– II. Title.

BR563.N4W55   1986   248.2'4'08996073   85-15829

ISBN 0-687-21698-2
(alk. paper)

The dream quoted on pages 12 and 128 is printed by permission of Richard H.
Cobble, Jr., Interdenominational Theological Center, Atlanta, Georgia.

The material from *God Struck Me Dead,* ed. by Clifton H. Johnson, is reprinted
by permission of the publisher. Copyright © 1969 United Church Press.

Chapter 5 is adapted from Anne Streaty Wimberly's "Spirituals as Symbolic
Expression," *The Journal of the Interdenominational Theological Center,* vol. 5 (Fall
1977). Used by permission.

Chapter 7 is adapted from Edward P. Wimberly's "The Healing Tradition of
the Black Church and Modern Science: A Model of Tradition," *The Journal of the
Interdenominational Theological Center,* vol. 11 (Fall 1983). Used by permission.

MANUFACTURED BY THE PARTHENON PRESS AT
NASHVILLE, TENNESSEE, UNITED STATES OF AMERICA

To our parents—
Valeska Streaty and the late Robert H. Streaty
and
Evelyn and Edgar V. Wimberly

ACKNOWLEDGMENTS

We began work on this book in 1979, and from the beginning many people have contributed to its development. Tremendous gratitude goes out to them from us, and we would like to acknowledge them at this time.

In the very early stages of the book, Dr. Manfred Hoffmann and Dr. Charles Gerkin at Candler School of Theology, Emory University, were very helpful by pointing to some of the theoretical problems of the manuscript. Dr. J. Deotis Roberts of Eastern Baptist Theological Seminary, Dr. Thomas J. Pugh of the Interdenominational Theological Center, and Dr. Major Jones of Gammon Theological Seminary were instrumental in providing financial resources for a sabbatical leave to complete research for the manuscript.

Dr. Howard J. Clinebell, the Institute of Religion and Wholeness at the School of Theology at Claremont, California, provided us with study facilities during our sabbatical. Dr. Burrell Dinkins and Dr. Trevor Grizzle, the School of Theology, Oral Roberts University, read the entire manuscript and made helpful comments. Dr. Thomas Hoyt, Hartford Theological Seminary, also read the manuscript and made helpful comments. Ms. Dorothy White, graduate student, and Mr. Lynn Nichols of the editorial department of Oral Roberts University edited the manuscript. Dr. James Buskirk, former Dean of the School of Theology, Oral Roberts University, made word processing and editing resources available through the university. Rev. Oon-chor Khoo, Oral Roberts

University and Mrs. Carolyn McCrary-Dennis, Interdenominational Theological Center, made bibliographical checks. We are very grateful for all of the selfless contributions of these persons and the many students at ITC and Oral Roberts who helped shape many of our ideas, especially Richard Cobble whose dreams we've used.

CONTENTS

PREFACE

Within Christian life and faith today, there is a renewal of meaning informed by the rediscovery of the transcendent, or supernatural, dimension. The supernatural involves a transcendent God who breaks into the natural order to encounter persons in life-changing ways. This dimension moves beyond naturalism, which perceives God as immanently participating in human growth through the natural process without a dramatic intervention to disrupt or speed up the natural flow of things. The rediscovery of the transcendent highlights the need for both the transcendent and immanent dimensions to be held in tension to avoid abuses of either extreme.

There has been an imbalance between the transcendent and immanent dimensions of the faith tradition in the interpretation of the experiences of persons, evidenced by limiting of the interpretation of faith experiences to current cultural symbols. These symbols, provided by technology and the human potential movement, cannot by themselves provide the necessary ingredients for a meaningful life for Christians. Contemporary symbols must be buttressed by the world views and images of the Judeo-Christian tradition that transmit not only images of wholeness, but also convey the power to become whole through God's intervention.

An important avenue exists within the black church and theological education from the black perspective to bring the transcendent dimension to bear on the faith experiences of persons. Through interpreting the conversion experiences of its foreparents and interfacing these interpretations with contemporary black experience, a renewed religious life evolves. The faith community attempts to live out its historical faith in its contemporary context. The recovery of a meaningful faith includes the discovery and the interpretation of God's liberating, holistic activity and power in the past and the discernment of how this same activity and power continue today. In other words, such a recovery requires a connection between the past and the present activities and power of God within Christian individuals and their communities. How, specifically, is this connection accomplished?

A dream of a black theology student provides a starting point. The dream was presented to a personality and religion class for confirmation of the religious significance that the student attributed to it.

I parked my car in a factory parking lot. I got out of the car and went into the factory. There was a conveyor belt where caskets were being moved up to a special room. I found myself on the conveyor belt face down going up to this room. When I arrived at the room a man met me. He said that he was a Jew. This man gave me a ticket receipt, and told me where to go next. I found myself back on the conveyor belt facing up this time on my back. When I got down to the bottom of the conveyor line, I saw a woman who asked me for a ticket, but I had no ticket. I had only the receipt for the ticket. I gave her the receipt, and then I proceeded into a room where the people were gathered in a circle to worship.

The manner by which the student was enabled to interpret the meaning of this dream for his life was a hermeneutical process. Hermeneutics refers to the interpretation and reinterpretation process that brings meaning to events in the here and now. Within this small seminary classroom, hermeneutics meant engaging in a holistic process of bringing supernatural and natural meaning to the dream experience so that its significance for the student's life could be plumbed. This involved five facets: Christian heritage and Scripture, modern psychology, cultural heritage, contemporary symbols, and the quality of the relationships in the classroom setting. While the complete analysis of this dream event will be carried out in chapter 7, it is important to speak of these five facets here.

The class and the student utilized their Christian heritage and Scripture as a way of taking seriously the historical witness of faith. As a hermeneutical task, this means of interpretation was a way of "seeing" the dream in the light of the Judeo-Christian tradition. Modern psychology informed an understanding of the psychological and spiritual significance of the dream. The dream was then reinterpreted in the light of the black Christian tradition and of the students' existential experience of God. Their experiences of God through contemporary images, symbols, and worship provided the fourth interpretive point of view. Throughout the interpretation and reinterpretation process, the atmosphere and the quality of relationships within the small class were influential components; combined with the other facets, the quality of class-student interactions linked personal meaning with communal meaning.

To state it in other terms, the recovery and renewal of a meaningful religious life and faith—belief in the continuity of God's activity and power in bringing about human wholeness—is a hermeneutical task. Life within the community of faith, whether past or present, must be interpreted and reinterpreted; and it must be done from a decidedly Christian perspective. Therefore, the hermeneutical task of contemporary Christian communities must take the Scriptures and the historical witness of faith communities seriously. No real renewal of faith and life in religious communities will take place without a dialogue with tradition.

Passing tradition on is not enough. The dynamic liberating activity of God that the Judeo-Christian tradition proclaims must be encountered within the images, symbols, worship, and stories of the faith communities. The Judeo-Christian tradition is not static. To declare it static and void of God's activity is to trivialize its potential for the growth and development of persons and communities. Some have tried to lessen the impact of tradition on the lives of people because it can restrict human freedom. As Howard Clinebell points out, however, the Judeo-Christian tradition contains within it growth-liberating factors as well as growth-inhibiting factors.[1]

Our task is to limit the growth-inhibiting factors of tradition and make the dynamic growth-liberating factors more available to others.

The world view undergirding tradition is an important aspect of the hermeneutical process. We define *world view* as the system of ideas, values, images, and symbols that give life meaning within a particular sociocultural setting. It is imperative that we pay close attention to the Judeo-Christian world view that undergirds our tradition. This world view helps contemporary faith communities interpret the dynamic liberating activity of God. But, with specific reference to the black church, there exists a world view that undergirds its past religious life and that has come to us by way of a tradition of the elders. This tradition includes recorded and oral affirmations of the the faith of slaves and ex-slaves. The slave narratives describing conversion experiences provide a rich resource for discovering this world view; and, for this reason, central attention will be given in this book to the conversion material recorded for and by black elders. Significant for our task is the fact that the symbolic world view that undergirds the narratives is Judeo-Christian enriched by African tradition.

The study of slave and ex-slave conversion experiences can help us understand how to relate hermeneutically the supernatural and natural dimensions of growth toward wholeness in the interpretive process. The world view of the slave tradition is holistic in that it encompasses the Judeo-Christian and African heritages and the particular ideas, values, images, symbols, and communal relationships that are unique to its cultural experiences of bondage. The experiences of conversion brought together transcendent, spiritual reality and natural, social reality. God's movement in the slaves' lives engendered a change in how they interpreted life and their response to God. This slave tradition provides an important guide to faith communities today in interpreting religious experience.

Notes

1. Howard Clinebell, *Growth Counseling* (Nashville: Abingdon Press, 1979), pp. 129-53.

Chapter 1

INTRODUCTION

The recovery and renewal of a meaningful faith today begins with our faith tradition. Tradition includes our biblical faith as well as our Christian heritage over the centuries. However, plumbing the depths of tradition for its relevance today requires a rigorous task of interpretation.

Tradition is the living faith of our ancestors, and this faith comes alive to us only when we bring to it our own subjective experiences, according to Jerome K. Del Pino, church historian and pastor,[1] who further states that "our forebears will have little to say to us if we do not impose our questions on their legacy." Following these suggestions, we have explored the contemporary significance of conversion in the slave tradition in the period of 1750–1930. This tradition took biblical faith seriously as well as its own interpretation of the faith tradition. Tradition includes the beliefs, values, and ideas relating to the perceived nature of reality and the perceived nature of human beings that informed the slave conversion experience. The idea system undergirding tradition and influencing the behavior of persons is often called a symbolic world view. Our concern is to examine the symbolic universe of black people in and out of bondage in America between 1750 and 1930. Its meaning and its function within its social context provide clues for recovering a meaningful life and faith today.

The exploration of the slave conversion tradition reveals images of human wholeness, a relational growth model undergirding the religious life of black Christians. These persons had a relationship to their past, their bodies, their minds, their environment, to others, to social institutions, and to God. They had the kind of spiritual and communal ties with one another that enabled them to grow personally as well as enable others to grow. Moreover, they saw growth in relational terms as vital in spite of the oppressive conditions of slavery and racism.

Hermeneutically, the relevance of the slave conversion experience lies in its images, processes, concepts, and ideas that give clues into God's liberating and holistic activity today. Conversion experiences performed the holistic function of facilitating growth.[2] The exploration of the holistic function helps us interpret our own religious experience today and recover a meaningful religious life and faith.

New Directions

Today there is a need for a world view larger than the science-based technological images of human potential held out by some segments of the secular world. Indeed, the world is more than physiological, psychic energy or mechanical and material elements alone. Building interpretive models of human and religious behavior exclusively on physical science analogies and imagery limits the scope of what it means to be human.

William James was aware of the shortcoming of basing interpretive models exclusively on the physical sciences. He operated out of a philosophical world view that enabled him to utilize psychological and theological categories.[3] He expanded his definition of the physical world to include the subconscious dimensions of human experience, but he transcended the physical analogies and images that existed during his time.[4] His model left room for the manifestation of the supernatural breaking into the natural.[5]

Unlike James, some theorists of religious experiences today seek to confine the transcendent and spiritual experiences of persons to naturalistic interpretations alone. The supernatural referent is removed. They theorize out of a scienced-based world view that sees the universe as self-contained with no supernatural or transcendent forces intervening or giving guidance in any way.[6] However, some segments of the scientific community are acknowledging that science rests on the metaphysical assumption that there is a natural realm of order; this natural orderliness is, however, a description of only one level of reality.[7]

These ideas currently being discussed in scientific circles represent a liberation from an exclusively secular view of science and open the door to transcendent, or supernatural, interpretations of religious experience that do not have to be in conflict with science. We can now affirm our faith heritage and a religio-symbolic world view that envisages God's transcendence and immanence in non-naturalistic as well as in naturalistic terms. We can build interpretive models of religious experience based on the Judeo-Christian tradition out of which we come. Moreover, salient behavioral science models that are consistent with a religio-symbolic viewpoint can be adapted to our interpretive models.

Anton Boisen, a disciple of James, looked at religious experience in its social context, as well as in its psychological and theological contexts.[8] This study will continue the trend represented by Boisen to put the religious experience in its social context. More precisely, this study will attempt to examine the conversion experiences of black Christians from within the psychological, theological, and sociocultural aspects of their world view as slave and ex-slave. The assumption of this approach is that personal experiences point to a wider social environment, and considering this social environment enables hermeneutics to be more inclusive and holistic.

Another noteworthy aspect of the study of slave/ex-slave conversion experiences is that a dichotomy between the natural and supernatural dimensions is not evident, consciously or unconsciously, in the conversion material. That is, the supernatural perspective used to describe conversion experiences in the black Christian tradition did not fracture or dichotomize experience. Rather, it brought a relational wholeness to life that enabled the slave to transcend slave status and be a real participant in life despite bondage. Thus, the study of the conversion experiences of slaves and ex-slaves challenges our hermeneutical task to become more interdisciplinary.

This study also contributes to the hermeneutical task of pastoral counseling identified by Charles V. Gerkin in his book on revisioning pastoral counseling in a hermeneutical mode.[9] Gerkin views the task of pastoral counseling as the interpretation and reinterpretation of human experience within a primarily Christian perspective. His Christian mode of interpretation includes dialogue with contemporary psychological modes of interpretation. Moreover, he feels that the pastoral counselor is a self-conscious representative of Christian forms of interpretation of human experience that are rooted in primordial images of the Christian understanding of the world. We feel that Gerkin has articulated our understanding of not only the task of pastoral counseling, but also the central task of ministry today in black churches and churches in general. Indeed, the contemporary task of ministry is to help people shape a meaningful response to life by drawing on the religio-symbolic images of the Christian tradition and the current images of the behavioral sciences. This interpretive-reinterpretive task takes place in every area of ministry from worship to social outreach.

This study also has implications for the way theology will be carried out in a postmodern age where people have become disenchanted with a world shaped by science-based technological images. Harvey Cox points out that postmodern theology will come not from western theologies but from the bottom up and from the periphery in.[10] He points out that a great inversion is taking place in theology: liberal theologies that have attempted to interpret Christianity in terms of a modern world view are now giving way to a postmodern age which will be characterized by folk religion, grass-roots piety, and popular religion. Thus, postmodern theology will emerge in dialogue with the disinherited and culturally dominated sectors of society, according to Cox.

Cox's conclusion about postmodern theology is also true for the interpretive-reinterpretive process in ministry. Neglected folk piety and religio-symbolic traditional images will have a significant place in the interpretation process. This study can provide direction for making folk piety and religio-symbolic images available to the whole church today.

The final significance of this work is in its contribution to understanding the role of women in postmodern theology. This role is highlighted throughout the study.

The Meaning of Conversion

The slave conversion experiences belong to a class of experiential phenomena called transcendent, transpersonal, and spiritual solitary experiences. In such experiences, normal everyday cognitive, perceptual, and visual laws of technical reasoning, consciousness, and awareness are temporarily suspended or disrupted. The person immediately becomes aware of the transcendent, spiritual dimension of reality, and this experience has profound implications for the person's life.

In the slave and ex-slave conversion tradition, the logical consistency in patterns of consciousness was temporarily disrupted, and this disruption created the possibility for apprehending new information that could radically alter the prior patterns of consciousness.

The radical shakeup in customary patterns of consciousness for the slave resulted from experiences coming from sources that were extrasensory, transpersonal, transcendent, and supernatural. The person felt encountered by something or someone outside the normal channels of consciousness. Once the encounter took place, normal technical reasoning and the communal interpretive mechanisms were reactivated. This form of revelation, as the slaves called it, had to be interpreted. The interpretive process involved logic as well as the interpretive tools provided by the social context.

Seven characteristics are suggested by the conversion experience. First, the normal vehicle for the conversion experiences of the slave and ex-slave was a mystical vision which was an inner experience occurring in a twilight or semiconscious state. Second, the message of the vision was usually conveyed in a stage drama and was acted out by characters taking specific roles. Third, the experiencer was a character in the drama, but was also an observer, simultaneously. Fourth, similar characters, images, and themes appeared in many of the reported experiences and had transforming significance and meaning for the convert's life. Fifth, the source of the new information was described as Christian and supernatural; yet, the communal world view helped shape the supernatural interpretation for the vision. Sixth, this world view helped the convert to find his or her place in the world. Seventh, and finally, the experience precipitated a radical turnaround in thinking and behavior which became nurtured and acted out in Christian community.

In many ways conversion experiences of slaves and ex-slaves reveal a level of faith and hermeneutical understanding that James Fowler calls conjunctive faith.[11] This is the fifth stage in his hierarchical faith stage model that is characterized by second naïveté in that religio-symbolic power is reunited with conceptual meanings. This stage is rarely achieved prior to mid-life and is an attempt to rework and reclaim one's past. There is an opening to the voice of the deeper self, and there is a recognition of the social unconscious. That is, the myth, ideal image, and values built firmly into one's self system by virtue of participation in a particular social class, religious tradition, and ethnic group come into full use in the religious life of the person. People in this stage are alive to paradox—the truth in apparent contradictions. There is a unification of opposites in experience and in the mind. There is a willingness to be open to new depths of religious experience, spirituality, and revelation. There is a concern and commitment to justice and to the growth of others. These persons have been grasped by the dynamic activity of the transcendent to which symbols and ritual point. These persons are participants in society and want to make contributions to their own group; yet such contributions are not limited to race or class.

The conversion narratives describe a process of life review that is closely related to Fowler's fifth faith stage. The slave recounts past history in ways that bring meaning to present life. Meaning came as a result of reshaping the past according to present experience.

In summary, the type of conversion experience described and defined above has many dimensions. It touches the whole person from his or her inner being to social and cultural aspects of the community's life.

Hermeneutics

Hermeneutics refers to the attempt to uncover the meaning of the existing literature of the past and to ascertain how this meaning can be applied to the life of Christian community today. This method includes the sources of data used and the manner in which one proceeds to analyze the data in the sources. The primary data for this study are slave narratives. There are generally two kinds. The first kind, autobiographical narrative, was written by or recorded for fugitive slaves who escaped bondage before its abolition, and was used in the antislavery effort. These autobiographical narratives included works of Sojourner Truth, Henry Bibb, William Wells Brown, Solomon Northrup, Josiah Henson, Moses Grandy, and James W. C. Pennington.

The second source of slave narratives was recorded after slavery was abolished as part of the Federal Writers' Project of the WPA in the 1930s. These narratives came directly from interviews with black people formerly in slavery and were recorded in a collection of nineteen volumes edited by George Rawich called *The American Slave: A Composite Autobiography* (Greenwood Press, 1972). These volumes have more than ten thousand pages and were recorded by numerous interviewers. The collection was placed in the Library of Congress in 1939. Visionary encounters are found scattered throughout the nineteen volumes, but many conversion encounters are found in the last volume of the set. These have been compiled in the Fisk University collection entitled *God Struck Me Dead: Religious Conversion Experiences of Ex-slaves*. Also, the biography of Harriet Tubman and the autobiography of Richard Allen are important sources.

Getting the necessary information from the data in the slave narrative material required two approaches. The first approach was to examine in detail about sixty conversion accounts and systematically record the repetitive themes and visual images that occur in them. This method is called the structural-functional-contextual method in folklore study.[12] The themes and images perform specific functions for each person experiencing them when the conversion encounter is placed in its psychological and sociocultural context.

Throughout the analysis of the conversion encounters, the subjective meaning of each experience was attended to because the meaning of the event for the person points to the symbol system, or world view, that undergirds the experience. From the subjective meaning of the experience, it was possible to draw inferences concerning the ideas, values, and theology of those persons experiencing the encounters when these experiences were put in their social context.

The concept of need emerged as the best concept for determining the functions of images and themes in individual conversion experiences. By *need* we are referring to conditions that must be satisfied within the person's life.

Moving from the past to the present required a second method. The hermeneutical method of engagement was chosen for this purpose.[13] This method enabled us to move from an analysis of the past to its significance for the present. This method is concerned to lift up (1) the central, dynamic activity of God in the past, (2) the continuation of this activity in communities of faith today, and (3) the impact of the dynamic activity of God on events and experiences in communities of faith.

The organizational structure of the chapters reflects the several methods described. In each chapter the needs manifested in the conversion experiences are explored. Following this exploration, the function that the conversion experience performed in response to the need is examined. Then there is a theoretical reflection on the issues that are raised by the particular chapter. Finally, the theological significance of the analysis for today's communities of faith is examined. Thus, the movement in each chapter has the following sequence: need, function, theoretical reflection, and hermeneutical significance for today.

Notes

1. Jerome King Del Pino, "Dual Ordination? No?" *Circuit Rider* (October 1982), p. 13.

2. This conclusion concerning the holistic function puts this study in the pragmatic tradition of psychology of religion. The pragmatic tradition is concerned whether or not the experience contributes to life. See James R. Scroggs and William T. Douglas, "Issues in the Psychology of Religious Conversion," in *Current Perspectives in Psychology of Religion*, H. Newton Maloney, ed. (Grand Rapids: Wm B. Eerdmans Publishing Co., 1977), pp. 256-58.

3. William James, *The Varieties of Religious Experience* (New York: The New American Library, Mentor Books, 1961, 3rd printing), pp. 172-73, 186-87, 190, 221.

4. E. Brooks Holifield points out the shift to naturalistic categories of power, energy, and force, i.e., a shift to the language of technology. See *A History of Pastoral Care in America: From Salvation to Self-Realization* (Nashville: Abingdon Press, 1983), p. 166.

5. James, *Varieties*, p. 393.

6. Yandall Woodfin, *With All Your Mind: A Christian Philosophy* (Nashville: Abingdon Press, 1980), p. 173.

7. See David Griffin, "Theology and the Rise of Modern Science," unpublished article, School of Theology at Claremont, Claremont, Calif., November 1982; and Woodfin, *With All Your Mind*, pp. 185, 189.

8. See *Exploration of the Inner World: A Study of Mental Disorder and Religious Experience* (Philadelphia: University of Pennsylvania Press, 1936), pp. 15-57. See also Hugh W. Sandborn, *Mental-Spiritual Health Models: An Analysis of Boisen, Hiltner and Clinebell* (Washington, D.C.: University Press of America, 1979), p. 17.

For descriptions of aesthetic experiences, see Abraham Maslow, *Religions, Values, and Peak-Experiences* (New York: Penguin Books, 1970); see also Linda Bourgue, *Social Correlations of Transcendental Experiences* (Ann Arbor: University Microfilms International, 1968). For a description of mystical experience and expansion of consciousness, see Wayne Oates, *The Psychology of Religion* (Waco, Texas: Word, 1973).

9. Charles V. Gerkin, *The Living Human Document: Revisioning Pastoral Counseling in a Hermeneutical Mode* (Nashville: Abingdon Press, 1984), p. 20.

10. Harvey Cox, *Religion in the Secular City: Toward a Postmodern Theology* (New York: Simon & Schuster, 1984), pp. 175-80.

11. James W. Fowler, *Stages of Faith: The Psychology of Human Development and the Quest for Meaning* (New York: Harper & Row Publishers, 1981), pp. 197-98.

12. Richard M. Dorson, ed., *Folklore and Folklife: An Introduction* (Chicago: University of Chicago Press, 1972), p. 34.

13. The hermeneutics of engagement is influenced by several people. Prominent is the work on hermeneutical engagement in Paul Hanson's *Dynamic Transcendence* (Philadelphia: Fortress Press, 1978), pp. 76-90. Other influences include the following: phenomenological hermeneutics associated with Paul Ricoeur—see Stanley T. Sutphin, *Options in Contemporary Theology* (Washington, D.C.: University Press of America, 1979), pp. 153-58; James W. Fowler's Stage 5 faith, *Stages of Faith*, pp. 184-98; and Charles Gerkin, *The Living Human Document*.

Chapter 2

THE NEED FOR SALVATION:
THEMES AND IMAGES

I was a great musician, and at times, after I had spent seasons at fasting and praying, I would get tired of it and go back to the ways of the world. You see, the devil knows how to tempt a man. . . .

God started on me when I was a little boy. I used to grieve a lot over my mother. She had been sold away from me and taken a long way off. One evening I was going through the woods to get the cows. I was walking along thinking about Mama and crying. Then a voice spoke to me and said, "Blessed art thou. An obedient child shall live out the fullness of his days" . . . But from this time on I thought more about God and my soul and started to praying as best I knew how. It went on this way until I was about grown. . . .

When God called me I had applied in hell, but my name wasn't on the roll. I saw a sharp-eyed looking man, and he seemed to be walking back and forth from one end of a workshop to the other and looking at a time book. I went to ask him if my name was in the book, and he snapped back, "No!" It was from here that God delivered my soul, turned me around, and gave me my orders.[1]

Each of the conversion visions studied for this book were explored in detail, and the personal needs expressed in the visions were recorded. Theological, psychological, and psychosocial aspects of personal needs were evident in each vision. Moreover, the images in the visions helped to pinpoint the major personal needs of the person and the function of the vision in meeting those needs.

Before devoting exclusive attention to the need for salvation expressed in the conversion visions, it is important to demonstrate briefly how each vision was analyzed and how we derived our conclusions. The above case will illustrate this analysis.

The first paragraph of the vision reveals a conflict between the spiritual interests and the material, or worldly, interests of the person. This conflict manifested itself from the time he was a small boy. It was exacerbated by the selling of his mother that separated them.

A voice from the deep came to him when he was a small boy grieving over his mother. It brought assurance that obedience would lead to a life of fullness. Obedience did not refer to being an obedient slave. Rather, it meant allowing God to work within him to bring wholeness. This is confirmed by the fact that he prayed more and paid more attention to spiritual things after hearing the voice.

His personal need for salvation from the inner conflict between his spiritual nature and the world was expressed dramatically in another part of his account not contained in the above excerpt. One day as he was plowing in the field he heard a voice behind a stump moaning for deliverance. He did not understand this incident at first, but God revealed to him that it was his soul. Although the voice appeared to be outside him, it was, rather, a projection of his inner struggle. The manifest need, then, in the narrative of this person's encounters with God was for personal salvation—the deliverance of his soul from hell.

Several images in the narrative support this conclusion. The image of the devil as tempter is evident. When he was called by God the image of "applying in hell" appeared. The image of "roll" as a record kept in hell in his narrative also supports our conclusion. He discovered his name was not on the roll book for hell, and it was then that God delivered his soul.

This brief analysis of the need for salvation is the manner in which we proceeded in each vision. We examined the needs expressed in the narrative by following closely the words and interpretation of the experiencer.

Further analysis of the narrative reveals that conversion was a dramatic event involving actors on a stage. The convert was a passive, but open, participant in the drama. God was the actor. The theme of salvation was then dramatically acted out. In this particular vision, it is not possible to determine whether the drama of salvation was happening or whether it had already taken place in the past. Regardless of the point of the conversion at the time of the vision, God was doing something significant in his life.

The stage-drama aspect of the vision was present in many of the conversion encounter visions.[2] Also, there were repetitive themes and images. These reveal different phases of the salvation visions as well as point to the importance of the drama for the growth of the person. The various themes and images in the conversion encounter visions led the person to holistic personality growth.[3]

Three phases of the vision can be discerned in the narrative. The first phase is the introduction or announcement of the need. This usually referred to a personal need. Then an agent was introduced to meet the need. In this case, the agent was a sharp-eyed man. The third phase was a concluding scene in which the need had been fulfilled. The three-phase drama is the structure that underlies the conversion vision that led the person to wholeness.

It must be emphasized that the personal need and its satisfaction took place within a social context. Thus, the repetitive themes and images point to larger processes that are communal in nature. The interpretation of the encounter and the way in which the person expressed the satisfaction of a need depended on symbols embedded in the slave tradition. Images of relational wholeness were also embedded in the social world view. Thus, isolating the inner dimensions and content of the conversion vision for examination is a theoretical necessity. The conversion experience, however, is a personal experience within a social context.

The Theme of Salvation

Salvation (soteria) in a biblical sense denotes personal deliverance and preservation as well as social deliverance from danger and apprehension.[4] The need for both personal and social liberation is evident in the conversion vision tradition. To illustrate the double aspect of the salvation need, we will examine the immediate needs surrounding the occurrence of the visionary experience.

Needs, or conditions requiring supply, always point to structures and patterns that supply the needs. In other words, needs always point to themes and images that are evident in the conversion visions. These structures, patterns, images, and themes were social mechanisms provided by the slave tradition to satisfy deep personal needs.

The First Phase—Spiritual Needs

The first phase of the conversion vision drama introduced the need. The most obvious need was deliverance, liberation, and freedom from a pervasive sense of personal sin.[5] Look back to the introductory case. The person said, "When God called me I had applied in hell . . . ." He obviously felt that his spirit was in bondage along with his body. He felt a deep need to be delivered from a sense of sin. Albert J. Raboteau, in *Slave Religion*, points out that a feeling of sinfulness and a vision of damnation often accompanied the conversion vision.[6] In the words of William James, the conversion visions studied here were of the twice-born nature, where the sense of personal sin was pervasive.[7]

Harriet Tubman is an example of this manifest need for spiritual salvation. Because of her death-defying trips to carry more than three hundred slaves to freedom, she has been called the Moses of her people.[8]

When Harriet was a young girl, her slave master hired her out to work for a family. Her job was to care for her new master's small child.[9] As a hired hand, she had to be maid by day and the child's nurse at night. She was given no instructions on how to do the job of a nurse or maid. Because she was inexperienced and very young, she was continually assaulted verbally and physically on the job. She would even be whipped if she was caught asleep by the bedside of the white child in the middle of the night. There was no real rest for her. The hiring family returned her to her original master because they said she wasn't worth the money. She was in poor health when she returned, and her mother had to nurse her back to life.

As soon as she was strong enough to work again, her slave master once again hired her out to a man whose brutality was extreme. Suffering from a brain injury inflicted by this new master, she would often need relief from work, but none came. Because of exhaustion, she was returned again to her owner, sick and unable to work. She lay in bed from Christmas to March. During this time she prayed continually for her master's conversion. She wanted God to change the man's heart. However, she changed her prayer when she heard she would be sent South by her master as soon as she was able to move. She prayed, "Lord, if you ain't never going to change dat man's heart, *kill him*, Lord, and take him out of de way, so he won't do no more mischief."[10] The next thing she knew, her master was dead, and he died a wicked man just as he had lived.

She was deeply remorseful for her death prayer for her owner. Angry and hurt deeply when she prayed it, she said she really didn't want him to die. "Oh, den it 'peared like I would give de world full of silver and gold, if I had it, to bring dat pore soul back, I would give *myself*; I would give eberything! But he was gone, I couldn't pray for him no more."[11]

She emerged from her illness and from her death prayer with a deeper spiritual need to be a companion of the Lord.

'Pears like, I prayed all de time . . . about my work, eberywhere; I was always talking to de Lord. When I went to the horse-trough to wash my face, and took up de water in my hands, I said, "Oh, Lord, wash me, make me clean." When I took up de towel to wipe my face and hands, I cried, "Oh, Lord, for Jesus' sake, wipe away all my sins!" When I took up de broom and began to sweep, I groaned, "Oh, Lord, whatsoebber sin dere be in my heart, sweep it out, Lord, clar and clean;" but I can't pray no more for pore ole master.[12]

Indeed, she had a deep awareness of her own need for salvation from herself. While we could excuse her bitterness toward her slave master by seeing sin exclusively as social oppression, it is obvious that Harriet was deeply convicted of her own sense of sinfulness. Her remorse could not be explained away by exclaiming that she was illiterate and uneducated. Nor could one dismiss her conviction by pointing to an inadequate theology taught by the slave master's religion. Rather, she had a conviction, a compelling belief, deep in her sinful soul about her own nature before God. Convinced of her unworthiness, she drew closer to God in confession and repentance, and it was to this need for forgiveness and spiritual liberation that God responded and freed her. It was out of this spiritual freedom that she decided to move toward her material, economic, and social freedom. It was after her experience of God's forgiveness that she was assured God would lead her and others in her race to freedom. It was at the moment of her spiritual liberation that she realized that social liberation from slavery was possible.

The sense of sin was also part of the conversion experiences of other slaves. This was true for the blacksmith James W. C. Pennington.[13] Sojourner Truth won her freedom by her own efforts, but she became aware of her sinful nature when she, like the Egyptians, desired slavery rather than freedom.[14] Josiah Henson said he had a clear perception of his own faults and of the sin that surrounded him.[15]

In summary it can be said that the need for liberation and deliverance from personal sin was very much a part of the slave narrative material published before and after slavery. This need for spiritual and personal salvation pointed to a world view that envisaged God as loving, caring, and forgiving. It saw God as one who personally came to deliver each person from his or her sin. The narrative material pointed to the fact that a person in bondage could experience sin and that the experience of personal sin was independent of external oppression. In the minds of people like Harriet Tubman, sin was a universal condition that only God could remove. The abolition of slavery would not remove the feeling of personal sinfulness. However, liberation from personal sin did open the eyes of people like Tubman to what God could do through them to fight for freedom from slavery.

Social Salvation

Freedom from slavery and salvation from personal sin are closely related themes in the slave material. They are intimately connected. As indicated in the life of Harriet Tubman, the desire for social deliverance burned deep in her breast along with the desire for personal salvation. Personal and social salvation mutually influenced each other in the slave tradition.

There is a difference in the emphasis on freedom in the narratives written before Emancipation and those recorded after Emancipation. Narratives recorded prior to Emancipation anticipated liberation, while those recorded in the 1930s were written after the dream of liberation was fulfilled. While the images and themes were essentially the same, the social context was different. It would be an error to suggest, however, that there was a separation between the spiritual and social deliverance in the minds of persons who recorded their narratives after slavery. These persons were children and teenagers when slavery was abolished, but they carried with them the memory scars of the cruelties perpetrated following slavery. It is safe to conclude that the narratives recorded at the two different times do not separate social and personal salvation.

The link between personal and social salvation can be visualized again in the dynamic figure of Harriet Tubman. Her reliance on the God who liberates the soul from hell parallels her belief in a God who liberates persons from material and social bondage. Before discussing Tubman, however, we want to present the freedom ambitions of James W. C. Pennington and Sojourner Truth.

Pennington's conversion came after he had escaped bondage and felt a strong need to help free the thousands of black folk still in slavery. Truth, on the other hand, was converted when she took steps to reenter slavery as a chattel slave because she did not like the loneliness of freedom. In short, we have three people in whose lives personal and social salvation were linked at different points. Tubman's spiritual conversion led to physical and social salvation. Pennington's material, physical, and social liberation led to his spiritual salvation. And Truth's inability to sustain her desire for material and social liberation led to her personal salvation. Let us look a little closer at Pennington and Truth.

James W. C. Pennington was the first black American to graduate from a European university.[16] He pastored a church in Brooklyn, New York, and led his congregation in some of the earliest nonviolent civil-rights demonstrations. He escaped slavery from the Eastern Shore of Maryland, the state that also gave the world Harriet Tubman. Reared in a close-knit family, he regretted having to leave behind his mother, father, six brothers, and four sisters in slavery. He was terribly frightened that they might be harmed as a result of his escape to freedom. In spite of this, he had to turn inner freedom into outer reality. Therefore, he ran away to freedom.

Yet, being free brought with it an inner turmoil. He could not forget those he left behind.

I began to contrast my condition with that of ten brothers and sisters I had left in slavery, and the condition of children I saw sitting around me on the Sabbath, with their pious teachers, with that of 700,000, now 800,440 slave children who had no means of Christian instruction.

He continued:

The theme was more powerful than any my mind had ever encountered before. It entered into the deep chambers of my soul, and stirred the most agitating emotions I had ever felt. The question was, what can I do for that vast body of suffering brotherhood I have left behind. To add to the weight and magnitude of the theme, I learnt for the first time, how many slaves there were. The question completely staggered my mind; and finding myself more and more borne down with it, until I was in an agony; I thought I would make it a subject of prayer to God, although prayer had not been my habit, having never attempted it but once.[17]

He prayed and it became apparent that he was a slave to another agent although he was a free man.

I not only prayed, but also fasted. It was while engaged thus, that my attention was seriously drawn to the fact that I was a lost sinner, and a slave to Satan; and soon I saw that I must make another escape from another tyrant. I did not by any means forget my fellow-bondmen, of whom I had been sorrowing so deeply, and travailing in spirit so earnestly; but I now saw that while man had been injuring me, I had been offending God; and that unless I ceased to offend him, I could not expect to have his sympathy in my wrongs; and moreover, that I could not be instrumental in eliciting his powerful aid in behalf of those for whom I mourned so deeply.[18]

Pennington's words are a remarkable summary of the relationship between personal salvation and socioeconomic liberation. Personal salvation was a prerequisite for receiving God's help in the liberation of his loved ones. The turmoil in his soul, initiated by a concern for his fellow human beings, led him to an awareness of his own need for salvation. He was converted shortly after becoming aware of his own sin, around 1828, and then he embarked on his antislavery work.

Sojourner Truth was in New York State about the same time as Pennington. She had run away to secure her freedom, and she was, indeed, free. But she found freedom lonely and desired to reenter slavery shortly before slavery was abolished in New York State in 1828. She thought of her companions (back in slavery) enjoying life in a carnival atmosphere on Sundays and holidays. In contrast, freedom was quiet, peaceful, and unexciting. She began to plot her return to slavery to experience the party atmosphere on holidays and on Sundays once again. She said she was looking back into Egypt as did the children of Israel in the wilderness.

That very day as she was making her effort to return to slavery, God appeared to her in a vision. She said God appeared with the suddenness of a flash of lightning. There was no place that God was not present. She became aware of God as her "almighty friend and ever-present help in time of trouble." Her unfaithfulness appeared before her and she wanted to hide herself from God in the bowels of the earth. She wanted to escape God's dreadful presence. She felt unworthy to speak to God, and she felt she needed someone worthy to stand between her and God because of her unworthiness. A friend did appear, and she felt refreshed. The vision brightened. She felt loved by the friend, yet she didn't know his name. When her desire to know who this person was

33

became insatiable, she discovered it was Jesus. She discovered that now she knew him personally as someone who loved and cared for her. She was no longer fearful of God; her heart was full of joy and gladness. She then proclaimed she could now see the world with the eyes of Jesus. She no longer desired to return to slavery. Thus, she began her ministry as a sojourner for the Lord.[19]

We find it significant that the supernatural conversion came at the point of her desire to return to slavery. Again the themes of personal salvation and social liberation are linked. She saw the hand of God intervening in her life when she was committing an act of self-destruction.

We have explored Pennington's and Sojourner Truth's conversions and have shown how personal salvation and social liberation were linked. Little effort so far has been taken to examine how God continued to manifest God's self after conversion as social liberation was pursued. Harriet Tubman's life and testimony guide at this point.

Harriet Tubman's biographer, who interviewed her directly for the biography, reports that she expected deliverance when she prayed. She trusted God completely since God had been proven completely trustworthy in her life. She trusted God so wholeheartedly that even if God chose not to deliver her, she would have accepted this as a divine decree.[20] Harriet trusted God to lead her as she made trip after trip into the South to liberate black people from bondage. She was never caught. God guided her, and she depended on God's visions to make a safe way. When people expressed astonishment at her courage and daring, she said:

Don't, I tell you, Missus, 'twant't me, twas de Lord! Jes' so long as he wanted to use me, he would take keer of me, an' when he didn't want me no longer, I was ready to go; I always tole him, I'm gwine to hole stiddy on to you, an' you've got to see me trou.[21]

What faith and what commitment she had! She was in touch with God's will for her life, and she kept her relationship with God continually. It was God's leadership and direction that led her as she helped God work out social liberation.

To this point, we have examined the need for freedom from sin as well as the need for freedom from social oppression. We have said that the visions had repeated themes that pointed to structures that met personal needs. The repeated themes have been awareness of sin, the awareness of the needs for personal salvation and social liberation. What are the structures that sought to meet these needs?

The Second Phase—Agents of Salvation

The second act of the conversion vision drama involved agents of God who guided the persons to personal salvation. This second phase introduced the major images of the drama. Supporting and lesser images helped to carry out this phase of the vision drama.

The major image in the conversion vision is Jesus. He brings soul salvation to the person. To illustrate this, we call your attention to the introductory case. A sharp-eyed man was looking at a time book. The time book was a supporting image helping to bring to light the man's concern about his soul's salvation. One is reminded here of the Negro spiritual, "So's I Can Write My Name," which refers to the book of eternal life in which the saints of the Lord have their names written.[22] The time book in the vision, however, referred to a place where lost souls' names are recorded. The major figure announced that the person's name was not in hell's time book and the person was converted. The major figure in the vision wasn't named, but this figure was said to be Jesus in many of the conversion visions. For example, Sojourner Truth called the central figure Jesus.[23] In her vision, Jesus appeared as a little man who guided the person through the maze of hell to safety in heaven.

Images here refer to symbols, in the forms of persons, places, or objects, that assist in the salvation drama. In addition to the figure that symbolized Jesus, visions contained images of heaven, hell, angels, the devil (Satan), pit, east, light, darkness, and the number 3. Other images appeared infrequently but often enough to be noteworthy: dog, road, tree, dove, city, mansions. Many of the images in the visions were biblical images. Moreover, these images also had roots in African tradition. The Bible and African heritage helped us discern some of the meanings of the visions.

Often, the meaning of an image and its function in the drama can be determined by the place it occupies in the drama. That is, its meaning can be discerned by whether it appeared in the first or second act of the drama.

Look at a typical example of a conversion vision.

In my vision I saw *hell* and the *devil*. I was crawling along a high brick wall, it seems, and it looked like I would fall into a dark, roaring *pit*. I looked away to the *east* and saw *Jesus*. He called to me and said, "Arise and follow me." He was standing in snow—the prettiest, whitest snow I have ever seen. I said, "Lord, I can't go, for that snow is too deep and cold." He commanded me the *third time* before I would go. I stepped out in it and it didn't seem a bit cold, nor did my feet sink into it. We traveled on *east* in a little *narrow path* and came to something that looked like a grape-arbor, and the snow was hanging down like icicles.

She continued:

I saw the *Lamb's book* of life and my name written in it. A voice spoke to me and said, "Whosoever my son sets *free* is free indeed. I give you a through *ticket* from hell to heaven. Go into yonder world and be not afraid, neither be dismayed, for you are an elect child and ready for the fold."[24] (italics added.)

We have italicized the key images in the vision. Consider their function in light of the phase of the drama. The need for soul salvation is expressed in the first phase of the vision. Crawling on the wall indicates she was near falling into the roaring pit. The images of hell (eternal damnation) and devil (hell's gatekeeper) point to her anxiety and need. The *pit* is the biblical term that refers to the grave and death.[25] Then, the drama moved to the second phase where Jesus was said to come from the east. East was a repetitive theme in the conversion visions, and it had biblical and African roots. It refers to the direction from which the sun and light come up onto the world.[26] Jesus comes from the east as a symbol of light bringing salvation. The experiencer was reluctant to follow Him at first. However, she was commanded *three times* to follow him. The number three symbolizes wholeness in

Scripture. For example, Jesus spent three days in hell before the resurrection. The number 3 was often a repetitive image in the conversion visions. Jesus led her on a *narrow path*. This symbolizes the familiar expression that the path to glory is narrow. Jesus functioned as her guide. She then saw her name written in the *Lamb's book*, and she was issued a ticket from hell to heaven. Her soul's salvation was completed when the voice of God said "Whosoever my son sets free is free indeed."

The images, then, assisted in the three-phase or three-act salvation drama. Other images could have served the same functions as those mentioned in this particular case. For example, an *angel* is the agent of God. A *snake* is often, but not exclusively, the agent of the *devil*. *Green pastures* refers to eternal life, and an *infant* refers to being spiritually reborn. More will be said about some of the images in the discussion of the final phase of the salvation drama, which is the completion of the salvation drama.

The Third Phase—Final Act of Salvation

It has been mentioned that the main function of the conversion vision was to meet the need for personal, spiritual salvation. The final phase of the salvation drama was the announcement of salvation. For example, in the most recently cited case, the woman saw her name written in the Lamb's book of life. Then, there was a proclamation by God, "Whosoever my son sets free is free, indeed," and she was given a "through ticket" from hell to heaven. Finally, she was told to make ready for the fold.

The final phase brought spiritual salvation to the person. Often, it pointed to a met need; it also pointed to a changed condition and a new perspective for the experiencer. Sojourner Truth said that physical reality appeared different to her; it was clad in new beauty, and she was able to see it through the eyes of Jesus.[27] One respondent said, "God delivered my soul, turned me around and gave me my orders."[28] Some persons even were healed of physical ailments following the visions.[29] Some, grieving over the loss of a loved one, found relief and comfort.[30] Others received their call to the ministry in the vision.[31]

The call to the ministry is an additional element present in the conversion in the examples mentioned. The person is set free to be a participant in ministry to others. Soul salvation demands a response. This has been illustrated by Harriet Tubman, Sojourner Truth, James W. C. Pennington, and countless others who felt called to service. Thus, the service aspect of salvation was expressed as freedom to be in ministry for others.

Since salvation has been shown to have personal, social, and service aspects, it can be said that salvation was a holistic experience in the slave tradition. It involved relatedness to God, to others, to self, and to physical reality including the environment and institutions. The conversion experience had implications for the holistic growth of persons. That is, the conversion vision of the slave indicated actual growth as well as the potential for growth toward God, self, others, and toward institutions and the environment.

Significant issues relative to conversion have been raised in the analysis. Salvation, conversion, growth, and liberation are major concepts that have been raised. Key theological issues are related to these concepts. The next section will raise these concerns.

The Theology of Conversion

Before turning to the hermeneutical concerns raised in this chapter it is important to reflect a little on the theology of conversion revealed in this analysis. The analysis of the theological need reflected in the conversion experience also demands theological reflection. Theological reflection sets the stage for hermeneutical reflection, which focuses theologically on God's activity in conversion. Theological reflection, however, lifts up other related theological issues.

Three critical theological issues are discussed in the literature pertinent to this discussion of conversion.[32] These issues are: (1) the relationship of conversion and salvation; (2) the order of salvation; and (3) whether or not salvation is a process or a sudden momentary change. A very brief discussion of each of these issues in the light of the conversion material will be presented here.

Salvation and conversion are linked in the slave conversion material, and it would be very difficult to understand conversion outside of the slave and ex-slave need for spiritual, social, and economic salvation and liberation. Salvation has been revealed as a spiritual and social liberation process initiated by God and occurring in the inner lives of persons as well as in the corporate community. In short, conversion has been revealed as a miniprocess within a larger macroprocess which involved the liberating activity of God within the community.

As a miniprocess, conversion was a turning of a person completely around in another direction. It began a process of sanctification where the person became a co-worker with God in bringing about personal and social holiness—that is, growth that was moral, spiritual, emotional, intellectual, interpersonal; growth in relationship to God, and to institutions; and growth toward full participation in life, committed to the welfare of others. Yet, this miniprocess was related to a larger or macroprocess where God was working out God's purposes.

This view of salvation as a mini- within a macroprocess is biblical. For example, Jesus' commission in Luke 9:11 links the preaching of the kingdom of God with the healing of those in need. Although the kingdom was not a nationalistic kingdom, it was nonetheless a kingdom where God was sovereign and ruled. Evidence of God's rule would be the healing of the lame, blind, and sick, the casting out of demons, and the conversion of persons. Moreover, this kingdom had personal as well as social dimensions; it also was present but yet to come. Biblically, personal and social salvation are linked, and the slaves and ex-slaves were consistent with biblical tradition.

The second issue concerns whether regeneration—the point at which God brings new life to the person—precedes, follows, or is simultaneous with the conversion. More definitely, the issue relates to whether or not the person was an active cause of his or her own salvation or whether it was a process initiated by God.

If the conversion process was a miniprocess within a macroprocess, then regeneration transcended individual control although the person had the freedom to align himself or herself with the movement of God. The person did not initiate God's activity in the world. God acts independently of human control, although people could respond to God's action. For example, the report of Sojourner Truth was that God initiated the action toward her, and she responded to God. Harriet Tubman, on the other hand, often sought God's help on her behalf. Yet, her seeking came as a result of her knowledge of God's macro-activity which she did not initiate.

In summary, then, it is not clear in the slave material whether regeneration followed, preceded or was simultaneous with conversion. What is clear is that people reported an experience that they believed God initiated.

The third issue addresses whether conversion was sudden or part of a process. Here again the macro- and miniprocess perspectives are key. The activity of God on the macrolevel was ongoing and continuous. This means that the activity of God had general purpose and direction for the slave. When the slave was in synchronicity with God's activity, specific direction and purpose were given to his or her existence. Having individual purpose and direction meant that the conversion was taking place.

The nature of conversion as a process was exemplified by Harriet Tubman. Her prayer for God to kill her slave master if God was not going to change his heart began a process of conversion. Her master died, and she felt tremendous guilt because her wish had become a reality. Although the two events, prayer and her master's death were not related, she felt that they were. Because of this guilt she came under conviction that she was responsible for her slave master's death. The need for forgiveness in her life was manifested, and God took a broom, so to speak, and whisked away her sin.

Characteristically, the slave narratives revealed that the conviction of sin was the beginning of conversion. Conversion was reported to involve the following: a conviction of sin, temporary withdrawal from community while God was working in the person's heart, regeneration, and reincorporation of the person into community through testifying to what God had done.

Although conversion was envisaged as a process by the slave, the moment of awareness of regeneration was sudden. The conversion was the sudden revelation of God's regenerating activity. Thus, it is clear that regeneration (the moment of new life) was in the context of a process of conviction, withdrawal, inner change, and reincorporation. Thus, conversion was viewed as a sudden change within a process.

Hermeneutical Concerns

Two steps have been involved in this chapter to this point. The first step was an analysis of the conversion encounter with the focus on the need for social and personal salvation. The second has been a theological reflection on major theological issues raised by the analysis. This latter step puts the analysis into its theological framework.

The third step is a continuation of the theological reflection. However, the reflection concerns itself with interpretation. That is, this step involves reflection on how the slaves and ex-slaves understood the central activity of God in their behalf. This sets the stage for the first dimension of the hermeneutics of engagement, which is discerning the central activity of God in tradition.[33] Dimension two—becoming aware of how the central activity of God is manifested in contemporary faith communities—and dimension three—courageously correlating God's activity with contemporary events—will be explored in the final chapter. The task here is to examine how the slaves and ex-slaves viewed God's central activity in their behalf.

The slaves and ex-slaves, both male and female, conceptualized God's central activity in their behalf as liberation from social oppression and personal sin. They were to grow in mind, body, and spirit, and in relationship to others, institutions, and God. The liberating work of God was continually reported to involve the forgiveness of sins and the working in behalf of the slaves to abolish slavery.

41

Key images accompanied the conceptualization of God's central activity in slavery, and these images helped give the slaves interpretive tools to understand the mini- and macromovement of God. The first image was sin, and this usually meant being at cross-purposes with God. The image corresponding to sin was God's forgiveness, understood as making things right again between the person and God. Other images expressing the liberating activity of God included Jesus as liberator, heaven as a place of reward for faithfulness to God's activities, angels who assisted in the liberation process, and light that expressed the essence of God's liberating activity in Jesus. These and other images discussed previously were used to express and interpret the central activity of God by the slave.

To examine the hermeneutical process itself in slave experience, we focus on the literary genre of the slave narrative. More precisely, the narrative allows us to examine the interpretation and reinterpretation process of the slave. As indicated in the introduction, many of the slaves were elderly at the time that they recorded their narratives, and this recording of their conversion experiences was itself a hermeneutical process. That is, it was a process that has been called life review[34] in which the slaves and ex-slaves reviewed their past and interpreted it anew. By life review we mean a personal and critical reflection process taking place in people beyond mid-life. In life review people structure and restructure the past in ways that reintegrate it into the present in meaningful ways. This review process is hermeneutical in that recounting one's story, restructuring it, and reinterpreting it is a self-assessment process that brings renewal, meaning, and identity. Thus, when the slaves and ex-slaves told their stories, they were doing life review, which renewed their lives in ways that gave them courage to face the future in their old age.

The life review of slaves, then, could be envisaged as a hermeneutical process through which their lives were restructured and reinterpreted in the light of the central activity of God. They reviewed God's historical relationship to their lives in ways that brought them to a new level of growth and wholeness.

Women were significantly represented in this life review and hermeneutical process. Sojourner Truth and Harriet Tubman were veritable examples. Countless lesser-known women also were crucial in this interpretation process.

Viewing the narratives as a hermeneutical process makes the study of them very important for our purposes. They give us a glimpse of how people reflect on their experiences in order to bring structure and meaning to them. Thus, it is possible not only to uncover what God was doing in their lives, but it is also possible to see how they conceptually integrated what God was doing. This insight helps to give shape to how people might respond to God's activity in faith communities today. Knowing how the slaves and ex-slaves as older adults utilized life review as a hermeneutical process points to the advanced stages of the hermeneutics of engagement to be examined in further detail in the final chapter.

So far we have implied that there is value in discovering how the slaves and ex-slaves understood the central liberating acts of God in their lives and in their community. We have also inferred that conceptualizing the life review process in this tradition is valuable to our model of the hermeneutics of engagement in which the past and the present are brought into dialogue. The question remains, Why are such approaches valuable for us today?

The answer to this question is that we live in a time when religious communities are realizing that conceptual, rational, and verifiable logic by themselves are inadequate for living a life in faith. There appears to be an awakening by the church and the theological community as a whole to the fact that the cognitive, rational, and critical cannot be separated from the imaginative, symbolic, and nonrational. Very few models are available that integrate the cognitive, rational, and critical with the imaginative, symbolic, and nonrational. There are extremes existing in many theological arenas. It is our belief that this false dichotomization does not exist in much of the

43

slave tradition of hermeneutics, and a holistic model of hermeneutics that unites both extremes can be developed from studying the slave conversion tradition.

The slaves and ex-slaves did, indeed, combine critical reflection with the power of the symbolic imagination in interpreting their faith or the way they leaned into life. James Fowler calls this ability to unite, second naïveté.[35] Second naïveté is not a precritical and naïve participation in the symbolically mediated faith of one's childhood religious tradition; nor is it conforming unquestioningly to the expectation and demands of religious tradition. Rather, it is a postcritical desire to allow the symbolic to take the initiative in one's life. There is an opening of the person to one's deeper self, a recognition of the role of paradox, images, and social symbols that make one who one is and assist in the rewriting of the past.[36]

Sojourner Truth, Harriet Tubman, and James W. C. Pennington were not naïve persons in their faith responding to social and environmental religious expectations. Their faith was a combination of their critical reflection on their own personal religious pilgrimage and the condition of black people in oppression. Their faith was in actuality one of responding to God's liberating activity and initiative in their lives, and they chose images and symbols from their religious communities that described and interpreted that activity. Thus, their hermeneutical process was neither immature nor inferior to the critical-rational approach. Rather, their faith combined opposites. It joined a critical evaluation of their past lives with the symbolic in a mature response to the central dynamic of their faith. Their faith and action on behalf of others can be seen as they interpreted and reinterpreted God's movement in their lives using images and symbols provided by their religious community.

The first step of the hermeneutics of engagement is to conceptualize how God was involved in a faith community of the past. In the slave tradition, God was visualized as a liberating God bringing wholeness to persons. They used selected images to interpret this liberating action of God, and reflecting on God's acts through life review was in itself hermeneutical. The value of the slave hermeneutics and their conception of God's liberating activity can assist us today to develop a mature hermeneutics of engagement in a time when the critical-rational dimension must be integrated with the imaginative-symbolic.

Notes

1. Clifton H. Johnson, ed. *God Struck Me Dead*, pp. 19-21.

2. Encounter vision is used as a descriptive term because not all of the encounters with God resulted in a dramatic turnaround of the person's life.

3. William James, *Varieties of Religious Experience* (New York: The New American Library, Mentor Books, 1961). The concern for the holistic growth of persons as a consequence of religious conversion closely relates to William James' pragmatic tradition in psychology of religion. An integrated personality has practical implications for the quality of life a person leads.

4. W. E. Vine, *An Expository Dictionary of New Testament Words* (Old Tappan, N.J.: Fleming H. Revell, 1966), p. 316.

5. E. Stanley Jones, *Conversion* (Nashville: Abingdon, MCMLIX). Jones points out that the fear of hell and its punishment is being shifted to the fear of hell in inner conflicts, in neuroses, in emotional breakdowns and tensions, and in an inner sense of guilt. This new sense of fear was evident in the slave conversion experiences.

6. (New York: Oxford University Press, 1978), pp. 267-71.

7. James, *Varieties*, pp. 140-41.

8. Sarah Bradford, *Harriet Tubman: The Moses of Her People* (New York: Corinth Books, 1961).

9. Ibid., pp. 17-25.

10. Ibid., p. 24.

11. Ibid.

12. Ibid., pp. 24-25.

13. James W. C. Pennington, *The Fugitive Blacksmith* (London: Charles Gilpin, 1849), published in *The American Negro: History and Literature*, W. L. Katz, ed. (New York: Arno Press and The New York Times, 1968), p. 53.

14. Sojourner Truth, *Narrative of Sojourner Truth* (Boston: J. B. Yerrington and Son, 1850), pp. 67-68.

15. Josiah Henson, "An Autobiography of the Reverend Josiah Henson," in *Four Fugitive Slave Narratives*, R. Wink et al., eds. (Reading, Mass.: Addison-Wesley, 1969), pp. 22-26.

16. Pennington, *The Fugitive Blacksmith*, pp. 50-57.

17. Ibid., pp. 51-52.

18. Ibid., p. 52.

19. Truth, *Narrative*, pp. 65-68.

20. Bradford, *Harriet Tubman*, p. 61.

21. Ibid.

22. Johnson, *God Struck Me Dead*, p. 59. The book of eternal life is called the Lamb's book.

23. Truth, *Narrative*, pp. 67-68.

24. Johnson, *God Struck Me Dead*, pp. 58-60.

25. William Piercy, *The Illustrated Bible Dictionary* (New York: E. P. Dutton, 1908), p. 694. See also Alan Richardson, ed., *A Theological Word Book of the Bible* (New York: Macmillan, 1951), pp. 106-7.

26. Piercy, *The Illustrated Bible Dictionary*, p. 224. For the African roots of the concept see Eugene Genovese, *Roll, Jordan Roll: The World the Slave Made* (New York: Vintage Books, 1972), p. 198.

27. Truth, *Narrative*, p. 68.

28. Johnson, *God Struck Me Dead*, p. 21.

29. Ibid., pp. 22-23.

30. Ibid., pp. 96-98, 153-63.

31. Ibid., pp. 15-18.

32. These critical issues have been raised by Cedric B. Johnson, and Newton H. Malony, *Christian Conversion: Biblical and Psychological Perspectives* (Grand Rapids, Mich.: Zondervan, 1982), pp. 103-10.

33. Paul Hanson, *Dynamic Transcendence* (Philadelphia: Fortress Press, 1978), pp. 76-90.

34. Anne Streaty Wimberly, "A Conceptual Model for Older Adult Curriculum Planning Processes Based on Normalization and Liberalism" (Ph.D. dissertation, Georgia State University, 1981), pp. 67-69.

35. James Fowler, *Stages of Faith: The Psychology of Human Development and the Quest for Meaning* (New York: Harper & Row Publishers, 1981), pp. 187-88.

36. Ibid., pp. 197-98.

Chapter 3

PSYCHOLOGICAL NEEDS AND THE CONVERSION VISIONS

It looked like I was having such a hard time. Everybody seemed to be getting along well but poor me. I told him so. I said, "Lord, it looks like you come to everybody's house but mine. . . . I have lived as it is becoming a poor widow woman to live and yet, Lord, it looks like I have a harder time than anybody." When I said this, something told me to turn around and look. I put my bundle down and looked towards the east part of the world. A voice spoke to me as plain as day, but it was inward and said, "I am a time-God working after the counsel of my own will. In due time I will bring all things to you. Remember and cause your heart to sing!"[1]

In the above case excerpt, the woman was telling God of deep emotional hurt because of the loss of her husband. She was grieving. Her major task was to let go of the deceased emotionally and to turn to building a new life without her loved one. She was at a point where she had to muster all the psychological and spiritual resources available to meet the demands of grief.

It was at the point of her deepest need emotionally and spiritually that she reached out to God; it was at this point that God was reaching out to her. God revealed God's self to her and she was comforted. It was in her grief that God suddenly broke into the natural grieving process and brought healing resources.

This chapter explores the psychological needs that are evident in the conversion encounters. These needs refer to personal problems that need solving. These personal problems emerge because of the natural psychological maturation of a person. They also arise as the result of facing threats to one's existence, such as the psychological need in these two periods for the person to muster the necessary coping skills to master the crisis of growth and the crisis of threat.

In the above case, reference is made to the grief and suffering caused by the death of a loved one. The woman had an emotional reaction to loss. The need was for her to work through her feelings of loss. She also needed to muster coping skills that would enable her to return to a meaningful life from which her loved one was missing. It was at the point of her need that God intervened to assist her in her natural grieving process and the tasks at hand.

As indicated in the last chapter, one of the major functions of the conversion vision encounter was to be a vehicle of God's deliverance from spiritual as well as social bondage. In the material to be analyzed here, the attention is not strictly focused on the liberation from sin or social and economic oppression. Rather, it focuses on psychological liberation or liberation of the growth possibilities in the midst of life crises. Indeed, conversion encounters have significant psychological consequences that need attention. That is, conversion also facilitated emotional and psychological healing, growth, and wholeness. It helped stimulate personality integration and greater use of personality coping skills.

Although no analysis of the social context will be attempted in this chapter, the social context is implied in the symbols the person chose to communicate and interpret what she heard. More than this, the support system that sustained her in her time of need was in the background. The support system provided interpersonal relationships as well as a coherent belief system that helped to channel the strong feelings.

Precipitating Events Surrounding the Conversion Vision

The conversion vision usually came at a crisis point or transition point. Threats from outside the person and inner changes introduced obstacles that could not be overcome easily. External threats causing severe difficulties and deep emotional reactions seemed to involve the loss of a loved one and the onset of illness. From within the person the transition periods (adolescence, young adulthood, and middle adulthood) marking stages of growth seemed to be the origin of internal crises.

In addition to transitional life crises and crises caused by external threats in the slave tradition there were emotional crises caused by personality integration. In addition to the normal stages of growth and the problems caused by external threats, there were crises caused when one's true self came into focus. The crisis came because the true self became the center of the whole personality. This often called for a process of reorientation. This also produced personal insecurity that had to be resolved. Thus personality integration, the focusing of personality, caused a crisis.

When discussing psychology and the growth of persons, conversion as a process becomes focal. That is, the shift is away from spiritual and material salvation, and the natural growth process of persons comes into focus. Conversion's relationship to the natural processes of growth and personality development are paramount. As we indicated in the last chapter, regeneration (the moment of new life) takes place within a conversion process. This conversion process has psychological growth dimensions.

Life Crises

The natural process of life involves facing threats of loss, real or imagined, to one's inner well-being. Usually, these threats of loss come as a result of facing situations that occur periodically throughout life. In the conversion vision material, the threatening situations were the loss of a loved one and the onset of illness. These life-threatening events presented opportunities for God's intervention into the natural processes of life to bring healing and sustenance. Some examples can be informative at this point.

The opening case in this chapter is an example of God's intervention in the grieving process to assist in the process.

Grieving involves accepting the fact of loss of a loved one, extricating oneself from the deceased, and beginning to live again. Psychologically, giving up the deceased involves expressing strong emotions that free the person from dependence on the deceased. These feelings include anger over abandonment by the deceased and God. Moreover, grieving also involves depression or mood dejection because one has lost part of one's self. People's feelings must be accepted by others and by God in order to work through the grieving process. If these feelings are not expressed, they become negative and work against the resolution of the grief. It was apparent in the case study of the grief-sufferer that God came to her with acceptance and comfort. In other words, the conversion vision was a vehicle of healing and wholeness. It was a reaffirmation of God's presence in her life and of God's desire to see her whole again following the loss. This case is an example of the need for liberation from psychological bondage to the deceased that was blocking her growth. God's love helped her face the tasks of grieving and expressing her anger toward being abandoned.

In other conversion visions, preparatory grief was the major psychological need of the person. Preparatory grief refers to the participation in the grief process prior to the loss of a loved one. All the emotional reactions exist as if the person were actually undergoing the grief process. An example of preparatory grief is found in an autobiographical account entitled "Slavery Was Hell Without Fires."[2]

In another vision, the woman was warned about something unnamed that was threatening. An image of a woman appeared, who called out to her three times. She was told to remain hidden in the yard so she could not be found. The vision was puzzling to her until she discovered that one of her daughter's close friends had died the very day of the vision. After the death, the meaning of the dream became clear to her.

Misery and loss were abundant during slavery, and this person's resources for dealing with another loss were meager. She needed help in order to cope with an additional loss. Therefore, she interpreted the meaning of the vision in the following manner:

But I was worried, because I didn't understand what J. meant by telling me to stay in the yard, etc. I prayed to God to show me what she meant. What she meant according to the spirit was that I am hidden and buried in Christ Jesus, and the world can't find me because the things of the spiritual are hidden from all save them that be born of the spirit. God made her come to tell me to hold fast to my faith.[3]

The vision brought hope and reassurance at a time when life was hard, and it prepared her for an additional loss. She was at a point where another loss would have threatened her own will to live, and therefore God intervened through a vision to liberate her emotional and spiritual coping mechanisms.

The role of significant others in her extended family also helped in her interpretation of the vision. The analysis of the role of significant others will be in chapter 4.

Another threatening event is the onset of sudden illness. As in the case of grieving, God also came to persons in their illnesses to bring healing and wholeness through conversion visions. One aspect of the case below is a vision, but another aspect is a dream in which God brought resources during sickness. Dreams function in similar ways to visions. The difference is that in dreams, one is fully asleep rather than partially asleep.

One night I remember I was sick, and the doctors said I couldn't live. During this time I lay on the bed with my arms folded. To my mind, in the spirit, a little silver pipe was let down from the top of the ceiling, and three angels came down. On this little silver pipe I could hear their little wings flapping, click, click.

The doctors wouldn't allow me to eat. I'd be so hungry and thirsty, and these little angels would come down loaded with food. They gave me water out of the little pipe. I could feel each drop on my tongue. They told me this was the water of life. Some nights I'd be so cold, and they would huddle close to me and warm me in my dreams.[4]

One aspect of being ill is feeling abandoned by God. In this illustration, the psychological need was for assurance of God's presence in sickness. God came through angels and brought healing and wholeness also. The angels assisted in nursing the person back to full health.

Illness and the loss of a loved one were precipitating events, and God was viewed as deciding to enter the process of living to bring healing and liberation. Illness and bereavement tend to be threats of loss outside the person. These threats are distinguished from problems caused by the transitions. For example, there are internal threats that are also opportunities for God's intervention in the growth of the person. These points of entry are periods of life transition within the life cycle, such as adolescence or adulthood. In these periods the person is moving from one stage of life to another. These changes are usually triggered by inner emotional, physical, and age maturation, and call for developing and learning new tasks.

Adolescence is that period when the person is making a transition from childhood to adulthood. It is marked by the onset of puberty, and the adolescent's major task is to establish an identity apart from the parents and to develop social and occupational skills to become self-sufficient in the world. The stage begins with the onset of puberty and lasts until age seventeen or eighteen.

Early adulthood represents the final stages in the process of separating from one's parents, establishing a personal identity, and preparing for a vocation. It is a point when one is ready to begin to put into practice all those psychological and social skills learned during adolescence. It is the period of settling down and establishing one's working and marital identity. This stage of life represents the ages of eighteen to thirty-five.

During both adolescence and early adulthood one's religious identity seemed to emerge in the conversion vision material. Below is an illustration of the life transition of adolescence. It must be remembered that the reality of slavery put limitations on the expression of psychological autonomy while causing vicious breaks with the family. However, following slavery autonomy from the family became more of a matter of choice.

God first spoke to me when I was a boy twelve or thirteen years old. I remember it as well as if it happened yesterday. I was on Winstead's

Hill, driving to town in a buggy. A voice spoke to me and said, "you must die and can't live." The thing scared me, and I looked about to see who spoke. About this time I heard singing. It was coming out of the east part of the world. I had never heard the words before, nor have I heard them since, but I remember them. It sounded like a multitude singing, and these are the words:

In all my Lord's appointed ways,
my journey I'll pursue.
Hinder me not, ye much-loved sins,
for I must not go with you![5]

This encounter was indeed a religious event occurring at an important transition point. The voice and the singing from the east indicate profound religious significance. East, as suggested previously, indicates the place of the rising sun. It signifies the direction from which salvation comes.

Abundant evidence in the conversion material indicates that adolescence was an important period for religious awakenings. Many of the youths were struggling with mastering their physical instincts, and religious awakening through visions had great potential for assisting them with this. Their spiritual awakening helped integrate their budding physical impulses.

Evidence also suggests that young adulthood was an important period for God's intervention into the growth process of persons. In early adulthood, the conversion experience often came as the result of the neglect of one's spiritual self. There was a deep sense of personal dissatisfaction with life. At the point of dissatisfaction, the spiritual dimension of the personality seemed to erupt, and it became the dominant and central dimension around which every other aspect of the personality was then organized. The primary psychological need in early adulthood was for the personality to find its center, which could then organize and integrate the whole personality.

It will be demonstrated later that social structure played an important role in life crises and life transitions. The visions did not do all the work. Social symbols, relationships, and ritual embodying resources worked along with what God was doing through dreams.

Personality Integration

While young adulthood and adolescence seemed to be the transition points at which conversion occurred, personality integration seemed to be more central. Thus, our task here is to explore the psychological function of personality integration that took place in the conversion visions.

Perhaps the best way to approach the theme of personality integration is to focus on the salvation theme of death and rebirth. By approaching conversion in this way, it is possible to envisage how it assisted personality integration. One experiencer heard a voice saying, "You got to die and can't live again."[6] This person became frightened because it meant physical dying. In fact, he said, "I felt myself dying." Then, he said, he turned his face to the east and saw himself in a vision. He said he was dressed up with a crown on his head and shoes on his feet and a snow-white robe on his body.

The theological significance of this vision was that the death of an old self preceded the birth of new self. The new self was symbolized by a crown and white robe, and both symbolize victory. The Negro spirituals also refer to victory in heaven in terms of crown, white robes, and shoes.[7] Thus, death of an old self and the birth of a new self had taken place in the vision. Regeneration (the point of new life) took place when the old self died and a new self, symbolized by white robe, crown, and shoes, was born. Shoes are poignant symbols because they were precious commodities to black people in slavery. Many reported being without them in the narratives.

Often, infants appear in the visions that came from the east.[8] The fact that infant and east are connected symbolically points to new life. Often the infant represented the second birth.

New birth was also symbolized in the visions through images of heaven. Mansions, white rooms, and gold are examples.

When I was killed dead I saw the devil and the fires of hell. The flames were blue and green. I left hell and came out pursued by the devil. God came to me as a little man. He came in my room and said, "Come on and go with me." He was dressed in dark, but later he came dressed in white and said, "Come, and I will show you paradise and the various kinds of mansions there." I saw the most beautiful rooms, all in white and gold. There was a stream flowing through every room. He said, "This is living water that flows from on high." He told me to taste it. It was the best-tasting water I ever drank.[9]

Indeed, God intervened to bring salvation from hell, but God also brought a new self. This was exemplified by the symbol of living water that referred to cleansing or to new life. The experiencer also reported a new life or change in his or her outlook as a result of the experience. This pointed to the fact that the new self or a spiritual self became the center around which all else was organized. Prior to the experience the self was organized around material and worldly things. However, after the experience, the person's life was organized around spiritual things. This did not necessarily imply a dualistic split between this world or other world. Rather, the world becomes organized around a new spiritual center. This is what is meant by personality integration.

Personality integration meant having a new center for the self; it also meant living a life that was congruent with that new center. In other words, personality integration referred to reorganizing one's life in behavioral and ethical ways congruent with the conversion experience. Personality integration meant turning from the worldly life of self-service to a life centered on God and to other's service.[10] Personality integration meant full participation in the community, serving others as a response to God's encountering the person. In other words, the conversion encounter contributed to holistic growth—growth toward self, others, God, and participation in community.

The Psychology of Conversion

We have explored the psychological needs of persons who underwent the conversion encounters. We discovered that God intervened in persons' lives to bring wholeness and healing during periods of bereavement, sickness, and at crucial points of life's transitions. We also explored the psychological functions of the conversion visions with regard to the personality being organized around a new center. Our conclusion is that the conversion experiences did have important psychological functions and contributed to the holistic growth of persons.

Critical issues need to be discussed with regard to the psychology of conversion. James R. Scroggs and William G. T. Douglass have raised many critical issues on the psychology of conversion.[11] By psychology of conversion, we mean psychological reflection on critical academic issues related to individual subjective experiences in the slave conversion tradition. This sets the stage for exploring the viewing of God's activity in psychological processes.

The Definition Issue

Is conversion a sudden, dramatic about-face or is it a process of gradual change? So far it can be said that the black conversion tradition emphasized the sudden, dramatic point of regeneration within the context of a process of growth.

The process dimensions can be discerned by looking at the distinct periods of slave conversion. Periods of preconversion and postconversion can be discerned in the conversion material.[12] For example, preconversion involves a point of growing awareness where a person experiences some inner tension or difficulty which needs resolution. In some cases reported here, the growing awareness was for assistance with transitional phases from one stage of growth to another. In other cases the growing awareness was for assistance with external threats which had the potential to block growth, such as the loss of a loved one or sickness.

Another growing awareness task was revealed when there was consciousness that there was a divided allegiance, and the personality needed to be integrated around a new center. For example, the death and rebirth theme alluded to earlier revealed an awareness that an allegiance of the self to a center that was not God had to die. The conversion vision dramatically pointed to the actual death of the old self so that a new self could be born around a new center.

The period of growing awareness in the conversion encounters was characterized by a sense of being under conviction. It was a sense that all was not well in one's inner life, and things needed to be changed. This period is called the incubation period. After this period there came a point of realization that God was present in one's life seeking to satisfy the expressed need of the person. Then, there came a period when the person realized what was taking place. Thus, the process of preconversion involved an incubation phase and a phase of realization.

Even though there was a sudden awareness of being converted in the slave tradition, this sudden awareness also was in the midst of a conversion process.

The definition issue also involves the question of whether or not conversion must be religious. More precisely, may a process such as brainwashing and psychotherapy be fundamentally the same as conversion? The similarity among psychotherapy, brainwashing, and conversion must be postponed until we discuss the role of community in conversion in chapter 4. However, the material does suggest that the black conversion tradition makes a distinction between Christian origins of the conversion experience and other experiences.

In summary, conversion in the slave material was sudden and dramatic as well as a process of growth.

The Pathology Issue

Is conversion pathological, abnormal, regressive, or a sign of mental illness or emotional instability? Let us examine the facts. First, people like Sojourner Truth, Harriet Tubman, James W. C. Pennington, and others who ran away before the end of slavery demonstrated remarkable mental and emotional stability. The conversion experience led them to full engagement with life rather than into isolation from life. Failure to participate in relationships characterizes regressive emotional instability.

Second, the persons who recorded their visions in the 1930s were obviously in their late 60s and early 70s at the youngest.

That is, they were children and teenagers at the time slavery was abolished, in 1864. There was no indication from the material that these persons were emotionally ill. In fact, they seem to have led full and productive lives, as the autobiographical sections of Clifton Johnson's book will support.[13]

The quality in the way the slave interviewees reviewed their lives also attests to the emotional stability of the slaves and ex-slaves. Life review refers to the ability of the person to review the past and to reinterpret it in the light of the present. In the slave narratives the slaves and ex-slaves reviewed their past and God's relationship to them in ways that brought meaning to the present. The slave narratives reflect their ability to draw inferences from complex past relationships using a reasoning power that reflected assimilation of cultural symbols and images. Such age-related formal reasoning is called crystallized intelligence.[14] Crystallized intelligence tends to increase gradually throughout the adult years, and it is evident in the narratives that the crystallized intelligence of the elders was functioning. There were no apparent blockages, emotional or neurological, hindering the life review process.

There was evidence of pathology, however, in the narratives. The vision experience and life of Nat Turner, who led a slave insurrection, revealed some tendency to go into isolation.[15] However, his tendency toward isolation existed before his vision. Moreover, his vision seemed to be from God, but his manner of interpreting his vision could have been faulty or even pathological, reflecting his frustration as a slave and his impatience with the fact that God had postponed revealing God's great mission to him.

Early in Turner's life, he had a sense that God had a special task for him, and his community affirmed this. However, as he grew older he became more and more impatient waiting for God to reveal God's purpose. He spent many hours alone fasting and praying, sometimes involving weeks at a time. He appeared as an aloof, austere, and mystical prophet; he avoided mixing in society and devoted himself to fasting and praying.[16] It appears to us that Nat's bent for social isolation, practiced over long periods of years, blunted the social dialogue and criticism needed for interpreting and reinterpreting deep inner religious experiences that were characteristic of most of the slave narratives. Thus, when he had his monumental vision and he saw the great conflict and blood, he could have been more isolated than ever. Even though he conducted his own praise meetings, these seemed to be occasions for delivering his apocalyptic vision rather than having the vision interpreted through dialogue with community. He possessed extraordinary gifts of the spirit—healing, prophecy, discernment. Yet, his penchant for social isolation, uncharacteristic of the other slave narrative material, leads us to conclude that Nat Turner misinterpreted the vision and that led him to the bringing of what he thought was God's judgment against slaveholders through murder. His inner battle and conflict seemed to be more the area of need for liberation. His inner war prevented him from hearing God's voice calling him to liberation of self first and others later. His social isolation was a key factor in his emotional stability.

This issue of pathology focuses on the importance of the social dimension of the conversion experience. Without the influence of society and culture in the interpreting process, the individual could become a victim of his or her own self.

The Convertible-Type Issue

This issue has to do with those who are psychologically likely to be converted and those who are not. More precisely, are those who are externally focused on others' expectations likely to be converted? The black narrative material is vast, and by no means did all the hundreds of persons interviewed report religious experiences. This could be indicative of lack of interest in religious material of some of the interviewers since some of the nineteen volumes hardly mention conversion at all. Nonetheless, a religious social environment did exist, and there was some social and religious expectation that a person be converted. Thus, those who psychologically derived identity from the expectations of others could have been coerced. This doesn't mean, however, that coercion was a critical factor for every person who was converted. It will be argued in a later chapter that culture must provide symbols to interpret deep inner feelings, but that these feelings do not find their origin in social expectations. Genuine conversion goes beyond social expectations.

The Ripe-Age Issue

Is conversion likely to occur at a certain age? The conversion material is affirmative on this question. We have seen that adolescence and young adulthood were the most likely periods of transition for the conversion experience to occur. Here again, however, it must be emphasized that this positive correlation is just a correlation. It cannot determine cause. In other words, life transitions cannot be said to have caused the religious experience. Rather, our conclusion is that God chose to intervene at these times to facilitate the process of growth.

Important also is the fact that the respondents were elderly people recalling their past experiences. Because of their increased crystallized intellectual ability, their recall of what happened many years before their old age can be trusted as accurate.

The Voluntaristic Issue

Is conversion the result of conscious striving and self-discipline or does it happen without willing it? The black conversion materials are unanimous in pointing to the involuntary origin of the conversion vision. However, this does not mean that persons did not seek it or fast or pray in hope of conversion. Indeed, many persons reported seeking conversions while others did not. Yet, the evidence is overwhelming that the persons experiencing conversion felt that the experience came from God and was beyond their control.

Hermeneutical Concerns

The psychology of conversion points to God's involvement in psychological processes. Hermeneutics within the psychological sphere focuses on how God's involvement in this sphere was interpreted. Examination of the faith community for insight into how it conceptualized the central activity of God is the first step in the hermeneutical process. In this chapter the central liberating activity of God was expanded from liberation from personal sin and social oppression to include the psychological sphere. More precisely, God's central activity was to liberate psychological processes to aid the growth of the person. Developmental transition periods and life crises presented the danger of arrested and regressed growth as well as an opportunity for maturation. These periods also represented opportunities for God to facilitate the growth process toward wholeness.

Improper centers for the organization of the personality presented the paramount danger to the slave personality. Improper centers become idolatrous norms around which the person evaluated his or her self-worth, relationships with others, and religious life. Idolatrous centers blocked holistic growth and therefore had to die before the true center of the self, God, took its place. Therefore, God's liberating activity at the depth of the slave's life removed the idol from the center of life, and God became the true center around which the whole life of the person was organized. It was out of this new center that one related to his or her mind and body, to others, to community, and to the culture. In other words, the removal of the idol facilitated growth in the person.

Images of psychological liberation also accompanied the conversion experience. Jesus Christ, the little man, angels, and the living water were all agents of God's liberating activity. Liberation images of new birth included mansions, white rooms, and new shoes. Other images impeded psychological and emotional liberation, such as the devil and the fires of hell. Yet, the image of God as liberator came through as central and more powerful than the devil.

The conversion visions reveal a deep hermeneutical process relating to what James Fowler calls the social unconscious. In the stage of second naïveté there is a confidence in and a coming to terms with the unconscious and a resubmission to the initiative of the symbolic.[17] We call the attention paid by the slaves and ex-slaves to the symbolic and unconscious "the unconscious hermeneutics." By this we mean that the interpretation-reinterpretation process has a technical, rational side, as well as a subliminal side functioning outside of consciousness. Subliminal, or unconscious, hermeneutics functions to resolve contradictions, paradoxes, riddles, and conflicts too complicated for the conscious mind.

An example of the functioning of the unconscious hermeneutics is the conversion vision of the person who was suffering from grief—introduced at the beginning of this chapter. Because of her grief she had regressed to a stage of ontological regression—regressing beyond the psycho-sexual stages of development to a place where God encounters and dialogues with the grief-sufferer. The dialogue is primarily unconscious, but the person often gets glimpses of the dialogue through conversion encounters. The encounter of this particular grief-sufferer took place in the east part of the world and she heard a voice from God that comforted her. It was at the conversion point that the question of why a good God would allow suffering was resolved. That is, the liberation activity of God at the depth of the unconscious communicated God's benevolent intent and loving presence in the midst of grief, and the grief-suffering was resolved. The conscious mind observed the process, but it was not a significant participant until after the resolution of grief was accomplished. The real meaning of suffering and God's goodness in spite of it took place at a subliminal level.

Slave conversions teach us today that significant growth insights are caught by the conscious mind. It is via unconscious archetypes or images that many significant insights emerge. Thus, the openness of the slave to his or her deeper self and the recognition of the role of symbol and revelation can add to our understanding of hermeneutics as more than a cognitive process alone. Indeed, our involvement in the central activity of God today can cause significant changes at the depth of our being which we catch by our conscious mind only after a deeper hermeneutics has occurred.

Throughout this chapter we have indicated that the images and themes recurring in the conversion visions were signs which pointed to a wider social context. Even though God was working at the depth of the person's life in periods of transition and life crises, how one perceived God's work depended on the social symbols permeating the culture of the slave community. Relationship to others and participation in communal religious activities were essential to bring meaning and perspective to significant subjective feelings and experiences.

Notes

1. Clifton Johnson, *God Struck Me Dead*, pp. 58-59.
2. Ibid., pp. 153-63.
3. Ibid., pp. 159-60.
4. Ibid., p. 123.
5. Ibid., p. 164.
6. Ibid., pp. 65-67.
7. John Lovell, *Black Songs: The Forge and the Flame* (New York: Macmillan, 1972), pp. 284-85.
8. Johnson, *God Struck Me Dead*, p. 91.
9. Ibid.
10. Ibid., pp. 19-21.
11. James R. Scroggs and William G. T. Douglass, "Issues in the Psychology of Religion," in *Current Perspectives in the Psychology of Religion*, H. Newton Maloney, ed. (Grand Rapids: Wm. B. Eerdmans, 1977), pp. 254-65.
12. Cedric B. Johnson and Newton H. Maloney, *Christian Conversion: Biblical and Psychological Perspectives* (Grand Rapids: Zondervan, 1982), pp. 71-72. They emphasize the phases of conversion.
13. Johnson, *God Struck Me Dead*, pp. 24-57, 68-90, 102-8, 116-20, 129-39.
14. Anne Streaty Wimberly, "A Conceptual Model for Older Adult Curriculum Planning Processes Based on Normalization and Liberation" (Ph.D. dissertation, Georgia State University, 1981), pp. 71-72.
15. See "Nat Turner's Confessions," in John Bayliss, ed., *Black Slave Narratives* (New York: Macmillan, 1970).
16. Stephen B. Oates, *The Fires of Jubilee: Nat Turner's Fierce Rebellion* (New York: Harper & Row Publishers, 1975), p. 27.
17. James Fowler, *Stages of Faith* (New York: Harper & Row Publishers, 1981), pp. 184-98.

Chapter 4

THE ROLE OF COMMUNITY IN CONVERSION: THE NEED FOR COMMUNITY

It has been indicated that the social context of the religious conversion is important. In fact, the world view and its symbols, images, and values undergirding the slave conversion tradition are dimensions of the social context. Another dimension includes the social vehicles through which the world view is brought to bear on the conversion experience prior to and after the encounter with God. The social context provided mechanisms that helped the experiencer interpret and integrate the experience into his or her life. The social vehicles enabled the experiencer to make a meaningful response to the experience. The need for liberation from bondage to personal sin and social oppression and the need for liberation from psychological blocks to personality growth had a social context. This context assisted the experiencer to appropriate the experience in holistic and growth-producing ways. The person's relationship to the community and to others is crucial for the person to interpret the conversion experience. This chapter will explore how the Christian community assisted in the conversion process and experience.

The slaves and ex-slaves were inheritors of the Reformation conviction that salvation was the result of a relationship with God. This orientation toward relationship along with the belief in an immanent and transcendent God, who encountered persons in the midst of life, enabled the person in and out of bondage to look inward to the heart to discern the work of

God's spirit there.[1] As the person turned inward to attend to God's working, the role of the Christian community, or those who had encountered God and were now responding to that encounter through caring for others, was (1) to form sustaining relationships with the experiencer before, during, and after the experience; (2) to attend to him or her by being a supportive presence; (3) to help the person interpret the practical implications of the conversion for everyday life; and (4) to create opportunities for the person to carry out the implications of the experience through participation in community. These four tasks or functions of the Christian community can be grouped into one function called communal presence, and this presence was the major form of care practiced by the black Christians between 1750–1930. In addition to the indigenous social context, there was the wider social context. The wider culture emphasized evangelical revivalism, and this evangelical revivalism encouraged the slave to trust his or her own inner experience of God.[2] Thus, slaves looked to their own experience with God and their own interpretations to work out a response system for those who were being converted. They paid little attention to the doctrines of the white slave masters who would use the Bible to support slavery. Rather, they trusted God's working in their hearts and the black caring community to help them plumb the depths of that experience for meaning.

There was an expressed need for help from the community by persons experiencing conversion. Their need was for caring by others who could help them make sense out of the experience. The next section focuses on this need.

The Need for a Caring Community

A religious experience has two aspects: positive and negative. It introduces to the person an opportunity and a danger. Some accounts in the slave narratives point to the fear that the religious experience introduced a challenge to the person's conscious world, and the tremendous experience drove persons to seek out others in order to find out what was going on inside them. One such experience happened to a twelve-year-old young woman when she felt something stirring in her soul. She heard a voice saying, "You never shall die a sinner." It also said, "You is jest in God's hands, and you must praise and bless God all the time." Then she reported the following experience:

Well, by and by I kinda got composed and went on up to the house. I didn't know nothin' 'bout it cept'n I felt funny and sorta light, and I went on in the house and told ole Aunt July. She said, "Chile, jest hold yo' peace, you done been left in God's hands." Well, you know I didn't know what that meant, now you know I was ignorant, jest young, you know. Aunt July told me to pray, pray. Well, I didn't know no more 'bout praying than this rock. I just cried, 'cause I had nobody to tell me nothing, and nobody what could 'splain the grace of God to me then.[3]

Since the young person lacked the skills to understand or interpret this experience, she suffered much anxiety, and therefore sought out her aunt hoping to find relief. The experience was more frightening than joyous. She was disappointed that her aunt could not do more for her. Disappointment led her toward others in the community. She demonstrated a need for a caring community.

This illustration points to the crucial role that one's social context plays in the interpretive process of deep inner emotional and religious experience. The experience precedes understanding. Often this understanding requires the help of the community. The religious experience needs to be interpreted in the language of the culture before that experience can become integrated into the life of that person. The role of culture is essential to understand the full implications of the religious experience.

As indicated, the black religious community provided language symbols for interpreting profound experiences on the emotional and religious level. In addition to this, spiritual guides were designated by the community to help persons make sense of what was taking place inside them. Unfortunately, Aunt July was not one of those persons although she did recognize what was taking place. Yet clearly a need was within the person to have someone to help her integrate the experience.

The Spiritual Guide

Slave culture often provided a spiritual guide to whom persons could go for understanding subjective experience. Albert Raboteau in his book *Slave Religion* discusses the role of spiritual guides in slavery.

Elder slaves, who had earned respect because of their wisdom or vision acted as spiritual mentors to their fellows. Frederick Douglass, for example, as a boy frequently sought the counsel of Uncle Charles Lawson, whom he called his spiritual father and "chief instructor in religious matters."[4]

Many such persons, both male and female, were provided by the community for interpreting inner experiences. Some were spiritual parents, prophets, and wise persons. They inspired a great deal of respect and were important religious leaders on the slave plantations. According to Raboteau, their duties were "advising on spiritual matters, opening and leading prayer meetings, counseling 'mourners,' sinners seeking conversion, and generally setting a Christian example for the slave."[5]

Closely linked to the spiritual guide was the medical practitioner on the plantation. W. E. B. DuBois in *The Souls of Black Folk* makes the link between spiritual guide and medical practitioner.

The chief remaining institution was the Priest or Medicine-man. He early appeared on the plantation and found his function as the healer of the sick, the interpreter of the Unknown, the comforter of the sorrowing, the supernatural avenger of wrong, and the one who rudely but picturesquely expressed the longing, disappointment, and resentment of a stolen and oppressed people.[6]

The fact that the person encountering God through a vision or dream turned to spiritual guides for interpretation is borne out by the slave narrative. Two examples will be given.

I do not remember how long I was in this state, for immediately I regained consciousness I began to shout and cry. I rushed to the house, my body all drenched in perspiration and my clothes torn from my body. I shouted the rest of the day and thought no more of the coming dance. I went to church on the following Sunday, having been directed in the spirit to an old preacher named Reverend Mason who, after hearing my testimony, reached me among his flock.[7]

Another example is:

When he finished speaking I came to myself, and it looked like I just wanted to kiss the very ground. I had never felt such a love before. Soon after this I went to Brother B. P. and told him what the Lord had done for me. He took me in and baptized me.[8]

There is some evidence that the black preacher could have functioned as scrutinizer and verifier, as well as interpreter of religious experiences. For example, among the Jamaican slaves, who were taken from the same general location in Africa as American slaves, a candidate for baptism had to have a vision or dream that was tested by the religious leaders.[9] In this role, the religious leaders would listen to the experience and decide whether or not it was genuine.

The person having a religious experience was not left to deal with that experience alone. Culture provided specific persons to whom the person could turn for interpretation, verification, and support.

The Religious Community

The religious community also performed a significant role in the religious experiences of persons. It was out of the interaction and activity of the community that the meaning came for interpreting the conversion experience. Therefore, the spiritual guide had to rely on a system of meaning that emerged from the community when interpreting the inner experiences of persons. Because of this function, the community formed an important dimension in the interpretive process.

Underlying the meaning universe, out of which interpretations came in the slave environment, was an assumption that the world of the spirit had a vital function to perform in the everyday lives of slaves. On this assumption, the task of the spirit world was to impact the physical reality of the slave in order to enable the slave to transcend that physical reality. Thus, much of the religious activity of the slave was focused upon enabling the spiritual world to impact their lives.

Certain patterns, or frequently repeated ways, of relating and interacting in the slave religious community facilitated or prepared the person for an encounter with the spirit realm. These patterns included a caring community and the mourner's bench. Within the small face-to-face setting, people related to one another in ways that prepared them for encountering God through images. These groups created an environment where persons felt the love, care, and concern of others. They also felt the expectations of others, and this helped them be receptive to the manifestation of the spirit world.

In the caring community persons who felt the need for conversion could find support. One ex-slave felt the need and sought out the church, where people prayed around him. He said: "I went on to church, and the brothers and sisters prayed around me. Then, like a flash, the power of God struck me. It seemed like something struck me in the top of my head and then went on out through the toes of my feet." He continued: "A voice said to me, "You are no longer a sinner. Go and tell the world what I have done for you."[10]

This person had been desiring conversion and felt the absence of a mother and father in his life. He wanted the parenting from his heavenly parent to be a substitute for his earthly parents. Therefore, he sought out a community that would accept and understand his yearnings.

Those who made up the community were willing to spend time with preparing themselves to be responsive to the divine. Raboteau says: "At the revival and prayer meetings, Christian members were willing to sing and pray over "mourners" all night long to help them come through to the Lord."[11]

One might think that a lot of coercive and negative persuasion of sinners went on at these meetings and that the person was brainwashed and had no choice. While there is evidence that this did happen,[12] there is also other evidence that points to the willingness of the caring community to respect the person's right to make up his or her own mind. The following excerpt illustrates the point that people were able to respect another's right to be alone in decision making.

I got so I felt heavy and burdened down again. My mother noticed it and asked me what was the matter. I told her I had heard a voice, and that I had been trying to pray. She clapped her hands. She said, "Pray on, daughter, for if the Master has started to working with you, he will not stop until he has freed your soul."[13]

The crucial point in this brief passage is that God begins to work on the soul of the person; and the role of the community, as represented by her mother, was to prepare the person to be receptive to it. Thus, the community performed its task better when the person had a stirring already taking place in his or her soul. In this context, the community performed the caring task as a way to create an environment for conversion to take place. The community aided God's work.

The caring role of the slave community can be envisaged also by the role the mourner's bench played in slave religion. Persons desiring to encounter God and to change their lives became the focus of the worshiping in the caring community, and this community gave as much concern and attention as needed to help the person concentrate on the task at hand. In those days sinners were called mourners, and the drama of the mourners and God's struggle with Satan unfolded before the caring community. It was felt that persons needed not only the help of God while wrestling with sin, but they needed also the help of caring others, while the soul was being purged of sin and Satan's influence. The following excerpt is illustrative of the role played by the mourner's bench and the caring community.

Preachers used to get up and preach and call moaners up to the moaner's bench. They would all kneel down and sometimes they would lay down on the floor, and the Christians would sing:
"Rassal Jacob, rassal as you did in the days of old,
Gonna rassal all night till broad day light
And ask God to bless my soul."
They would call for moaners the first night, and moaners would come up for two and three nights waiting to feel something, or to hear something. Sometimes they would walk way out in the woods after getting religion. They would get to rolling and shouting and tell everybody that they had found Jesus and they would shout and shout, and sometimes they would knock the preacher and deacon down shouting.[14]

Thus, the role of the caring community was to support the person when God was working and relating to him or her. They were to be a communal, relational presence.

Belief Systems

Part of the meaning universe out of which interpretations of the conversion experience came was a set of theological beliefs and values concerning the importance of the conversion experience.

In the slave Christian's world view, certain beliefs about religious experience were assigned priority. For example, the sinner was expected to have to descend to the depths of the lonesome valley.[15] This belief related to the death and rebirth theme. The person descended into hell prior to conversion. In fact, this was the experience of many; that is, conscious physical discomfort and emotional turmoil preceded conversion. Because so many described their experience beginning with a period of turmoil, the cultural belief system of the slave generalized this as the norm.

Since so many persons experienced the transformational impact of images on their lives, a belief system developed that made heartfelt religion central. Therefore, a truly religious person would, in the slave Christian's mind, have an experience of the spiritual realm. One ex-slave said, "Nobody can talk about the religion of God unless they've had a religious experience in it."[16] In some regions persons had to have a certain experience in order to be considered religious. For example, one person said: "In parts of Georgia they say that if a person has not hung over hell on a spider web that that person has not been converted."[17] Another person said the following about the centrality of experienced religion.

All has to be born of de Spirit to become chilluns of God. Romans, Chap. 6, 'lows something like dis: "He dat is dead in sin, how is it dat he can continue sin." Dat tell us dat every man, white or black, is de child of God. And it is Christ dat is buried in baptism, and we shall be buried in like manner. If Christ did not rise, den our preaching is in vain. And if we is not born agin, why den we is lost and our preaching is in vain.[18]

In the above quotation it is clear that the folk belief of the slave concerning conversion was theologically sound. The belief was that persons had to be twice born, a biblical belief, in order to be considered a believer.

Slave beliefs helped the process of converting the experience into an active status in the life of the slave and ex-slave. The expectation of being born twice by encountering God not only supported the person undergoing the conversion but also gave him or her some conceptual tools for interpreting what was happening deep within.

In addition to providing a system for interpretation, the belief system included prescribed methods of preparing oneself for an encounter with the divine that included corporate as well as individual acts. These included fasting and praying, meditation, spending nights at the graveyard, going to the mourning bench, and ring shouting. Ring shouting was the formation of a ring of worshipers who would dance and shout while moving counterclockwise in a circle. This was often believed to assist in the preparation of conversion.[19]

The Sociology of Conversion

Indigenous world views and spiritual guides performed an important role in the conversion experience. Religious functionaries, cultural practices, and beliefs assisted in the preparation of the person for the impacting of the spiritual dimension on the world of physical, conscious reality. While the communal practices did stir great emotions, the real transformation of persons was wrought by the vision. However, the concern of others helped to focus the soon-to-be-converted upon what was taking place within them. The community and the guide were essential in enabling the conversion vision to bring about important changes in the person's life.

This chapter raised critical sociological issues which must now be addressed. The sociology of conversion refers to the examination of critical sociological issues that relate to the role of the community in conversion.

Was the supportive Christian community influential in helping to shape the convert's response to the vision since the community persons were present at critical and crucial turning points?[20] The answer to this question is yes. Indeed, persons were vulnerable following an encounter with God, and the quality of the communal relational presence and the quality of the social symbols for translating the experience definitely influenced the person's response. In very real ways the religious experience, although inward and personal, pushed the person toward community. It was expected that the community would influence the response to the conversion experience.

The influence of the community was evident in that persons often sought out community to help them to understand and to interpret the experience. It was also true that the community was attuned to the inner workings of God in a person's life, and it was ready to respond appropriately. Moreover, the community provided spiritual guides who recognized the importance of assisting people at crucial points in their religious experiences.

Another question has to do with the quality of the influence that the community has on the vulnerable experiencer. More precisely, was the slave open to being brainwashed or to a social influence process, such as indoctrination? Indeed, the experiencer *was* vulnerable, and therefore brainwashing, or a process of indoctrination by psychological manipulation to change beliefs, *was* possible.

Moreover, social influence could have shaped the person's response. The real point here is that the conversion experiencers reported being in an environment of respect and acceptance. The community was present and attended to the inner happenings. The communal relational presence reported by the respondents was usually in cooperation with what God was doing rather than an imposition of doctrine or beliefs on the experience. There was a dialogue between the experiencer, God, and the community. Of course, there are examples of imposition of rigid doctrinal standards and expectations on the experiencer, yet the quality of communal presence in many cases showed respect for the person's right to appropriate personally what God was doing with him or her. Communal relational presence helped to protect the person from rigid communal expectations. In other words, personal freedom was not generally abridged in an atmosphere of communal relational presence. The respect for a person's ability to make decisions about his or her life was maintained within the caring community.

Another related issue has to do with whether or not a person's deficiency in or lack of affectional bonds with significant others influenced the religious conversion.[21] Indeed, a person may have had a deficit in the area of relatedness to significant others, as in the case with Aunt July mentioned at the onset of this chapter. Such a deficit would make the person more vulnerable to social influence, and therefore, it would be difficult to distinguish whether the person was converted because of social expectations or because of something genuinely taking place inside the person. The dominant expectation of the slave and ex-slave environment, however, was that something genuine had taken place within the person. In the examples cited above, which are representative, the Christian slave community saw its role as cooperating with and assisting what God was doing in the person through the Holy Spirit. Indeed, conversion was not expected to be cultural or produced because of social expectations, but it was hoped that conversion was the result of a saving relationship with Jesus Christ.

The final issue has to do with the role of community in the incorporation of the person into a new community.[22] Baptism, a symbol of the dying and rising with Christ, was the community's rite of passage of the person into Christian community. It symbolized the inward change and the acceptance by the community that the person was judged ready to be part of the Christian community. The denominational influence of the Baptists can be seen here, but the significance of baptism, or full immersion, of the person was important also to non-Baptist denominations including black Methodism.

The social context had a very significant role to play in the slave conversion experience. However, the conversion was neither cultural nor social in origin. It was initiated by God. Culture helped interpret and give shape to it. Indeed, the social context was significant in helping the conversion vision to produce holistic growth.

The examination of the sociology of conversion sets the stage for exploring the role of community in the hermeneutical process. Social reality provides interpretive tools which are the foundation of hermeneutics.

Hermeneutical Concerns

The central, dynamic activity of God discerned in this chapter was the liberating work of God in enabling the community of faith to participate in the wholeness process with individuals. Although God worked through personal encounters with individuals, God also worked through community to assist the person toward wholeness. It was natural for the experiencer to seek out community because of the need for communal support in the time of great inner turmoil, and God facilitated the use of the faith community to assist the person. Therefore, God was also in the community of faith bringing about wholeness.

This chapter revealed that the hermeneutical process in the slave and ex-slave community was communal. It was not a formal theological process in that the interpretation-reinter-pretation did not take place in abstract thinking. The faith community's hermeneutics was a communal, participatory process of mutual storytelling, drawing on images indigenous to the particular culture. The experiencer brought his or her experience to the community in the form of a story. The community listened to the story to ascertain whether or not the story was consistent with other stories heard in the community of faith. If the story was analogous to other stories shared in the community, then the vision and its interpretation were communally confirmed. Thus, the hermeneutical process was the interpretation and reinterpretation of experience via a model of communal-analogy-storytelling-listening.

God's liberating activity in the life of the community of faith used the medium of "communal analogy of the storytelling-listening." That is, what God did in the life of one person was checked out against other similar acts of God within the faith community. Moreover, it was God's incarnational presence assisting in this process of analogy storytelling-listening that completed the hermeneutical process. As the person told his or her story and as the community listened, God was at work in this process.

Although the communal-analogy-storytelling-listening hermeneutical model was not an abstract intellectual theological exercise following systematic categories and logic, it cannot be labeled as theologically inferior. Rather, it can be visualized as a very complex holistic thinking process embodying the rational, intuitive, relational, and feeling dimensions similar to Stage 5 thinking in Fowler's *Stages of Faith*. More precisely, the communal hermeneutics followed the method of coherence in that the story was critically analyzed by the community for its correspondence to other stories of conversion within the faith community. Yet, the checking was done in a manner that preserved in tension the rational, feeling, and spiritual dimensions of the conversion experience.

It is possible for us to learn not only from the communal-analogy-storytelling-listening model of the slave and ex-slave community, but also from the way in which the community of faith facilitated novelty and innovation in the hermeneutical process. That is to say, persons were integrated into a preexisting world view, but did this preclude the potential for forming new meanings? Our answer is that the respect that the community of faith had for the experiencer and the community of faith's tendency to shy away from indoctrination meant that new meaning was possible.

Preexistent universes are only partially given.[23] Although the reality of a preexisting world for a conversion experiencer might seem objective and fixed, new meanings are possible which contribute to the wholeness process of the experiencer and of the community of faith. Thus, in the mutual analogous storytelling-listening process, the existing meaning universes were fed by new experiences. Thus, there was a mutual feedback system where both preexisting meaning universe and the world view of the experiencer were enriched. Both the experiencer and the community of faith were expanded.

Another dimension of the hermeneutical process can be envisaged by examining the sources of images the faith community used to help in the communal-analogy-storytelling-listening process. The sources of the image were the slave and ex-slave's African heritage and the Bible. It was clear that the slaves and ex-slaves were not historical critical scholars in the academic sense of examining scriptures and historical documents. Rather, they learned from African traditions and the Bible through oral tradition. Yet, in the transmission of oral tradition there is a hermeneutical process called "projected meaning." The original meaning of a selected dimension of written tradition requires historical and critical academic tools. However, oral tradition picks up on projected meaning of texts and unwritten stories that transcend the original meaning. Oral tradition picks up the universal meaning of the written and unwritten tradition.[24] Oral tradition catches the projected meaning or universal meaning and creatively relates it to a specific context. Thus, the slaves and ex-slaves caught the projected meaning of the African world and the biblical world and innovatively used them to discern the activity of God in their midst.

The model of communal-analogy-storytelling-listening and catching the projected meaning through oral tradition gives us a glimpse of how hermeneutics worked in the slave and ex-slave environment. For them God was present and involved in all life including the thought processes of hermeneutics, and the community also played an essential role in this interpretation and reinterpretation process.

Notes

1. Albert Raboteau, *Slave Religion* (New York: Oxford University Press, 1978), p. 177.
2. Seventeenth- and eighteenth-century American revivalism was characterized by rational analysis and discernment of the soul's state. However, the slave community did not emphasize rational analysis

as much as it did the actual experience and whether or not the experience of the convert was similar to the experiences of others. Thus, existential comparison was more central than rational analysis. For a description of seventeenth- and eighteenth-century rational analysis of evangelical revivalism, see Brooks Holifield, *History of Pastoral Care in America: From Salvation to Self-Realization* (Nashville: Abingdon Press, 1983), p. 69.

3. George Rawich, ed. *The American Slave: A Composite Autobiography*, vol. 18: Unwritten History of Slavery (Westport, Conn.: Greenwood Press, 1971), pp. 163-64.

4. Raboteau, *Slave Religion*, p. 238.

5. Ibid.

6. W. E. B. DuBois, *The Souls of Black Folk* (Greenwich, Conn.: Fawcett Publications, 1961), p. 144.

7. Clifton Johnson, *God Struck Me Dead*, p. 101.

8. Ibid., p. 67.

9. Raboteau, *Slave Religion*, p. 29.

10. Johnson, *God Struck Me Dead*, p. 45.

11. Raboteau, *Slave Religion*, p. 255.

12. Johnson, *God Struck Me Dead*, pp. 123, 126.

13. Ibid., p. 169.

14. Rawich, *The American Slave*, vol. 18, pp. 48-49.

15. Raboteau, *Slave Religion*, pp. 253-54.

16. Johnson, *God Struck Me Dead*, p. 144.

17. Newbell Puckett, *Folk Beliefs of the Southern Negro* (Chapel Hill: University of North Carolina Press, 1926), p. 542.

18. George Rawich, ed., *The American Slave*, vol. 2, South Carolina Narratives, Parts I and II (Westport, Conn.: Greenwood Press, 1972), p. 84.

19. Raboteau, *Slave Religion*, p. 69.

20. Cedric B. Johnson and Newton H. Malony, *Christian Conversion: Biblical and Psychological Perspectives* (Grand Rapids: Zondervan, 1982), p. 26.

21. Ibid., p. 29.

22. Ibid., p. 36.

23. Stanley T. Sutphin, *Options in Contemporary Theology* (Washington, D.C.: University Press of America, 1979), p. 149.

24. Ibid., p. 157.

Chapter 5

SUSTAINING RELIGIOUS EXPERIENCE: THE NEED FOR CULTURAL EXPRESSION

The conversion experience did not reveal a need to have the conversion encounter renewed on an occasional basis. Yet, chapter 4 revealed the need of the experiencer for community. One role of community is to help keep alive the original religious experiences through ritual. Often cultural creations such as songs embody the themes, images, and symbols that help keep the original religious experience before the community. The Negro spirituals have served to meet this need for renewal.

Spirituals as Symbolic Expression

Images that appear to the person undergoing the religious experience are not once and for all, final, or one-time events. Rather, they often become reservoirs from which cultural expressions such as folklore, myths, art, and music are created. Experiences on the spiritual and psychic plane are not just isolated events taking place in one person, but they are often social events occurring simultaneously in more than one person. In this regard, the movement of the spiritual realm often manifests itself in whole communities, and the result is that collective images are created that bring forth meaningful symbols that can be used for creating culture.

It was out of the collective manifestation of the images that the Negro spiritual came. As the slave narratives have indicated, many of the Negro spirituals arose out of specific circumstances in particular settings in response to concrete needs. Indeed, one person may have encountered the images, but these images often expressed the heartfelt striving of others, and therefore became part of socially shared symbols. Thus, when the person encountered images, these images often became part of the shared symbols of the community giving a sense of meaning to all who were part of that communal family.

The importance of the study of the symbols and images expressed in the Negro spirituals is that spirituals are the music of the slaves and symbolize the slaves' need for ultimate truth and meaning amidst oppression. They are the representations of the striving of a transplanted people to come to terms with unfamiliar circumstances and to establish new identities in degrading conditions.

In the following discussion, the nature of the images appearing in the spirituals will be examined. The basic message of this chapter is that the spirituals are symbols put to music which point to the original religious experiences of a group, and participation in the singing of these songs puts persons into direct contact with the social, historical, and religious sources that gave rise to the symbols in the first place. In other words, the images in the spirituals are not merely images; they are images that have the power to affect the singer in profound ways; the spirituals are vehicles through which the original religious experience of a people was renewed. Thus, spirituals represent a need to sustain what God did and renew God's activity through cultural expression.

The Image of the Hero

When the slaves came to these shores, they were in desperate need of someone or something greater than themselves or any other human being. They needed something with which they could merge in order to derive strength for living. They did not need false gods or human substitutes. They needed something eternal, not temporary; infinite, not finite; and everlasting, not perishable. This something had to be a liberator, one who could conquer evil and defeat death. In other words, the slave had a need for a transcendent, heroic being.

The soul sought an image that could convey a power that was victorious and transcendent over evil. Where could such a symbol be found to fulfill such an enormous task? It was from the Christian Bible that the symbolic representations emerged. It was in the soul's encountering God in the world of the Hebrew that caught the fancy of the slave. In the words of Howard Thurman: "The Jewish concept of life . . . made a profound impression on this group of people, who were themselves in bondage. God was at work in all history: He manifested himself in certain specific acts that seemed to be over and above the historic process itself."[1]

The slaves found their hero or savior in God. God became the heroic archetype or image. But more than this, God's power to release those in bondage was invested in the personages of Old Testament heroes such as Moses, Daniel, and Joshua. And it was these heroes who appeared in spirituals such as "Go Down, Moses," "Didn't My Lawd Deliver Daniel?" and "Joshua Fit de Battle of Jericho." It is clear that the soul in its wandering found an analogous or parallel experience with Israel and drew upon the biblical images to help the slave make sense out of his or her existence.

Images Represented by Numbers

Numbers or emblematic material appeared quite often in Negro spirituals as they did in the slave conversion experiences. It is obvious that for the slave, numbers had deeper meanings or referred to something beyond a specifically designated, manifest meaning in a particular context. Indeed, spirituals were often thought to have double meanings; one for the specific context, and the other for expressing the strivings of a people for ultimate truth and meaning. On one level, the spirituals had specific, known functions, such as increasing fellowship among believers, calling slaves to the secret meeting for worship, or planning ways of taking their leave out of the view of the master. Beyond this, they also had a latent or unrecognized function of charting the soul's search for ultimate meaning. The effort here will be confined to exploring the latent function of numbers to produce meaning in the lives of the slave.

The number three was of specific significance to the slave. It had a religious meaning, from our point of view, since it appeared frequently in the conversion experiences of the slaves. Sometimes a slave would hear a voice calling three times as in the biblical story of Samuel in the Old Testament.[2] In other instances, the parallel is clear between Jesus' stay in the earth, or hell, for three days prior to the resurrection, on the one hand, and the three days turmoil and agony of the slaves during conversion, on the other.[3] It can be concluded, then, that the number three pointed to the manifestation of God's work in the lives of persons moving toward rebirth and renewal of the soul. More than this, this number also indicated that the true self, the one related to God, was emerging; and it was whole.

The number four in ancient mythology had the same religious connotation as the number three, according to Jung.[4] These two numbers are sometimes combined in the Negro spiritual as illustrated by "Oh! What a Beautiful City"; the slave sang about twelve gates—three in the east, three in the west, three in the north, and three in the south—or four sets of three:

> Oh! What a beautiful city!
> Oh! What a beautiful city!
> Oh! What a beautiful city!
> Twelve gates-a to the city, Hallelu!

Notice also the repeating of the first three lines of the song within the four-line refrain. Thus, even the musical form conforms to the religious intent of the number. Consider another stanza of the song that has the religious symbol four:

> My Lord built-a dat city,
> Said it was just-a fo' square;
> Wanted all-a you sinners
> To meet Him in-a de air;
> 'cause He built twelve gates-a to de city-a, Hallelu!

The argument for the religious nature of numbers can be enhanced by further reference to the image of the city. The city often has maternal implications.[5] If, then, the city represents psychologically the mother's womb, as does the earth, then there may be a parallel between this song and the fact that Jesus spent three days in the womb, or mother earth, prior to his resurrection or his second birth. The appearance of the numbers three and four with the image of the city may refer to the psychological and theological potential for rebirth for the slave, or it may refer to the fact that the second birth had already occurred and that the persons singing the spiritual were already whole persons. This kind of speculation gives some glimpse into the soul of the slave and points to the ability of the soul to enable persons to transcend cultural circumstances.

The Sun and Wheels

The sun and the wheel are significant images that refer to the depth and importance of the ultimate meaning in the life of the slave. The sun often symbolized the power and majesty of the Godhead that uplifted and sent light to the soul. The religious significance of the sun for the slave can also be envisaged in the dominant emphasis upon the direction "east" in the conversion experience. The religious power or the light which shone in darkness always came from the east and had religious significance for the slave.

The spiritual "Watch That Sun, How Steady It Runs" ("Live a-Humble") is one example of the importance of the sun to slaves:

> Watch that Sun, how steady it runs,
> Don't let it catch you with your work undone.

The sun also appears in the spiritual "Let Us Break Bread Together":

> Let us break bread together on our knees;
> Let us break bread together on our knees.
> When I fall on my knees, with my face to the rising sun,
> Oh, Lord, have mercy on me.

As a symbol related to the sun, the wheel represented for the slave a desire for wholeness, for a centered, integrated self, and for perfect harmony. As in ancient mythology,[6] the wheel often signified the healing of the soul as well as the movement of the soul, or self, to its fulfillment. This particular image appears in the spiritual "Ezek'el Saw de Wheel," which was inspired by the Old Testament visions of the prophet Ezekiel. The Israelites and Ezekiel were dispossessed people. In their exile, they searched for a purpose for their existence—to discover who they were and where they were going, as well as to affirm that they indeed counted for something. It was Ezekiel's vision of the wheel that brought their answer and their hope.

It is not known whether the slaves were fully cognizant of the intricacy of the vision as told in the Bible. Yet, it is clear from the reading of the slave narratives that they held their secret meetings out of sight and sound of the master so that such identification with the Israelite children's struggle for liberation could take place. These narratives reveal that they knew they were dispossessed people like the Israelites. Certainly, it is clear that they identified with Ezekiel's vision, and thereby incorporated it as their own symbolic expression of hope for rediscovering their identities and their purpose for being.

The above statement is not to imply that the identification with the Israelites was all conscious. The thesis is that the soul went a-wandering one night looking for images and fell upon the images of an oppressed people of long ago. Thus, the conscious and unconscious processes combined to make this identification.

The Rock Image

The spiritual, "Elijah Rock," exemplifies the attempt by black people to derive meaning from stones:

> Elijah rock, shout! shout!
> Elijah rock, comin' up Lord.
> Elijah rock, shout, shout!
> Elijah rock, comin' up Lord!

Satan's a liar and a conjur' too;
If you don't watch out he'll conjur you.
If I could I surely would
Just stand on the rock where Moses
    stood.

There are frequent references to conjuring in the slave narratives. Conjurers were often the workers of magic and manipulators of the spirit world. Some mention is made concerning how the conjuring powers could work upon the slave without having any significant influence on the master. In this context, many of the slaves were aware of the limitations of the conjurer's powers when it came to combating the forces of evil. Thus, the slaves were in need of something more steadfast, something superior to the conjurer.

The rock was the image the soul of the slave chose from nature to symbolize its striving for steadfastness and the unchangeable. The rock symbolized that power in the universe which could hold fast and sustain in spite of the forces of evil. It was through it that God's power worked to firm up a sure foundation to life.

It is not known from which testament the spiritual "Elijah Rock" came. In the Old Testament story, Elisha relied on the strength of Elijah (II Kings 2:9-12). Before Elijah's death, Elisha's last request was that he would be allowed to inherit a double share of Elijah's spirit. In this sense, Elijah as a "rock" was a lasting spirit, influencing and girding the life of Elisha.

Both Elijah and Moses appeared on a mountain in the New Testament story of Jesus and his disciples Peter and James (Matt. 17:1-3). In this story, the disciples became aware that Elijah was to come to make all things new and that he had, in fact, already come in the person of John the Baptist. One may conjecture that the mountain on which Elijah and Moses stood was considered the "rock." On the other hand, Elijah, was an eternal symbol which may have been combined with the knowledge of Moses and the stone tablets containing the Ten Commandments. Both explanations would at least in part explain the words of the spiritual, "Just stand on the rock where Moses stood."

The rock then had significance for the slave; it symbolized

the powers of the universe that held fast against the forces of evil. Not the conjurer's power or even Satan could overcome the power of God.

Fire and Water

The image of fire has a clear connection with the slave's African past, and it signifies life, warmth, growth, and the ground of natural existence. Thus, the soul could wander back into the slave's ancestral past to find the image of fire. However, the ancestral image of fire merged with the biblical image of fire, which meant the burning away of sins or cleansing of sin. Thus, the soul of the slave was able to seek out images from at least two primary sources—racial history and biblical history—and integrate them within their specific cultural context in order to help make persons' lives meaningful.

The fire was a redeeming element for the slave. The burning away of sins made possible the regeneration of life—the restoration of life to its proper relationship with God. Two specific examples of the slave's use of fire as symbolic material in spirituals are found in the spirituals "God's Gonna Set Dis Worl' on Fire" and "Ev'ry Time I Feel the Spirit."

Water also implied regeneration. Water has always been significant in the lives of black people and has often meant cleansing and regeneration. For the slave the Deity was often found in the living water, and baptism meant shedding the old self and putting on the new self. This view can be seen in the spirituals "Chilly Water" and "Wade in the Water." "Deep River" is another illustration of the significance of water.

Animal Motifs

Meaning often comes from identifying with the physical side of one's existence. Theologically, the slaves derived much hope from the fact that God took on the form of a human to experience the limitations of the human existence. Thus, for the slave, God had his human side, and the identification with this human side through Jesus gave the slave hope. The slave understood that God knew what it meant to be imprisoned in one's physical existence. The slave derived comfort from this knowledge.

How the slave derived hope from God's physical existence can be envisaged in the significance of animals in their religion. Animals are often part of the symbols of religion because they lift up the human, instinctual side of the spiritual dimension. Often animals are interchanged with God as a way to emphasize God's human side. This is evident in the spiritual that identified God as a suffering lamb. Spirituals such as "Lis'en to de Lam's," "De Ol' Sheep Done Know de Road," "Little Lamb, Little Innocent Lamb," and "Done Foun' My Los' Sheep" exemplify this use of the animal motif. These spirituals point to the paradox of God's existence, divine and human, as well as to God's suffering. A suffering God made it easier for the slave to approach God and to know God understood and cared for them.

Animals, then, helped make God more personal for the slave. The soul went in search of an image that could convey God's loving care to the slave, and he or she found a suffering God. But more than a suffering God, the slave found an able God. God suffered in order to be believable and to demonstrate how to live in this world; yet God was still divine, having the power to hold the forces of evil in check.

The Anthropology of Conversion

The anthropology of conversion explores conversion in the light of cultural sources. A brief analysis of the cultural sources of the slave conversion tradition points to the role of culture in hermeneutics.

The ability of the soul to encounter images that point to profound dimensions of life has been remarkable in the case of the slave. The images came from the slave's ancestral past, from history in general, and from the Bible. Beyond this, the soul was able to integrate these different histories into a coherent image to be drawn upon by the slave. Moreover, the image was not a private possession of the individual; it had the power to manifest itself simultaneously to other persons, thus laying the foundation for shared symbolic expressions such as the spirituals. In such expressions, the spirituals represented the quest of the slave for meaning and purpose in life.

Much discussion exists concerning whether the images in the spirituals were influenced more by African and racial sources than by other sources. This is an important debate; however, it is clear that the soul was not limited to racial history alone for its images. It encountered images of God's spirit wherever they could be found in human history. Sometimes the images sought to engage the soul, and the soul sought to engage the images. This mutual seeking took place with people everywhere. Thus images in the spirituals are both racial as well as general, particular as well as universal.

Hermeneutical Concerns

In chapter 4, the liberating activity of God was revealed as working in the communal-analogy-storytelling-listening model to bring personal wholeness. God's role in this model related directly to the interaction between the conversion vision experiencer and the principal interpreters and reinterpreters in the faith community. This chapter has examined another step in the hermeneutical process—involving how cultural symbols and images of God's central liberating activity are made available to the total community and to future generations. This chapter has revealed the relationship between culture and conversion. Here we will explore the cultural dimensions of the hermeneutical process. Culture here refers to the ritual and ceremonial life of a community of faith that transmits and celebrates the crucial events and values around which its whole life is organized.

The central dynamic act of God revealed in this chapter is the liberating work of God that helped the faith community express, through cultural mediums, what God did to bring human wholeness. Here the central hermeneutical task is to ascertain what God did at the level of culture to help the faith community express God's liberating work. Through the cultural medium of ritual—which includes music, instruments, art, patterns for body movement, symbols, images, values and language—God enabled the faith community to express what God did to bring wholeness to persons. It was through the cultural expression of ritual that the central liberating acts of God were made available to the wider community and to future generations of the faith community. It was also through ritual that the central events of the faith community were reinforced.

Some examination of this cultural hermeneutical process is in order. Cultural hermeneutics refers to the legitimating function that articulates and reiterates a system of meaning existing in a faith community.[7] Legitimating functions are those that justify the presence of the existing meaning systems and the reinforcement of this meaning through repetitive reenactment within the community. Legitimation is normative in that it provides the justification and rationale for existing practices and behavior that take place in the faith community.[8]

The Negro spiritual was used continually in the ritual life of the slave and ex-slave community. It embodied the expression of God's central liberating activity. It embodied the rationale for why the faith community gathered, and it justified the community's existence. Thus, the meaning system and world view embodied in the Negro spiritual performed a legitimating function. It was through ritual that the values and events embodied in the Negro spiritual were expressed. Hermeneutically, then, the singing of spirituals in worship formed a foundation for the interpretation-reinterpretation process with a given universe of meaning. Thus, the Negro spiritual contained within it an all-embracing frame of reference which embodied the faith community's reason for being. When the faith community sang the Negro spiritual in worship they reencountered the original event and experience that gave the initial purpose for its existence. In the singing of the Negro spiritual, the slave and ex-slave reencountered the liberating God of human wholeness. Thus, they experienced anew justification of their purpose in the faith community.

Succinctly, cultural hermeneutics refers to the communal frame of reference out of which the community of faith interpreted and reinterpreted its experiences in the light of the central liberating act of God. Cultural hermeneutics must be related to the other dimensions of hermeneutics discussed in previous chapters; namely, unconscious hermeneutics, communal-analogy-storytelling-listening hermeneutics, world view hermeneutics, the hermeneutics of life review, and the hermeneutics of engagement. These must be visualized within cultural hermeneutics. These other levels of hermeneutics were possible only because a level of meaning existed which justified all other levels of hermeneutics. There was, therefore, an objective level of meaning rooted in the continuing liberating activity of God which made multi-level hermeneutics possible.

We indicated that God was involved in helping the faith community express through cultural medium what God did in that community. God's role in the creation of the Negro spiritual was affirmed by pointing to the fact that similar songs appeared in different areas of the community. Thus, revelation had its personal as well as communal dimensions, and it was through its communal dimension that God's revelation became cultural expression. By its very nature, communal revelation by God required communal expression. Thus, the Negro spiritual was born as the result of God's liberating and revelatory activity because this activity demanded cultural expression.

The fact that God's liberating activity on behalf of others demands expression links hermeneutics and evangelism. Drawing persons who are not in the community of faith into its theological world view and community is a dimension of evangelism. By evangelism, we mean communicating God's central liberating activity in human wholeness to those who are either on the periphery of the faith community or who are outside the faith community. Evangelizing slaves and ex-slaves was part of the faith community's ritual life as well as its communal-analogy-storytelling-listening model. There was no way for those who were not part of the community of faith not to be evangelized if they came in contact with the worship life of the community of faith. They were drawn into the process of interpretation-reinterpretation taking place in the ritual life of the slave and ex-slave community of faith.

Culture is usually visualized as a human creation in response to human need. This chapter has revealed that God was also involved in the creation of culture. The Negro spiritual as a cultural expression was initiated by God's revelation.

Notes

1. Howard Thurman, *Deep River* (New York: Harper & Brothers, 1955), p. 13.

2. First Samuel 3:3-9 illustrates this from the Old Testament. See also Clifton Johnson, *God Struck Me Dead*, p. 20.

3. Ibid.

4. Carl Jung, *Man and His Symbols* (New York: Dell Publishing Co., 1964), p. 62.

5. See p. 35 of this volume.

6. For a discussion of the significance of the wheel in ancient mythology see Philip Wheelwright, *The Burning Fountain: A Study in the Language of Symbolism* (Bloomington: Indiana University Press, 1954), p. 123.

7. For a discussion of how ritual reinforces existing meaning, see Hans Mol, *Identity and the Sacred* (New York: The Free Press, 1976), pp. 233-45.

8. For the normative dimension of legitimation, see Peter Berger and Thomas Luckmann, *The Social Construction of Reality* (New York: Doubleday, 1967), pp. 92-104.

Chapter 6

THE PSYCHOSOCIAL WORLD VIEW
AND CONVERSION: THE NEED FOR
MEANING

We have addressed the theological, the personal, and the
social needs with which the conversion experiences were
concerned. We have concluded that each vision revealed the
need for social and personal salvation when examined from a
theological perspective. From a psychological perspective
each vision also revealed certain psychological needs which it
sought to fulfill. From a sociological perspective the need for
community was paramount. In addition to these theological,
psychological, and sociological needs, the vision sought to
satisfy certain psychosocial needs. Psychosocial needs are
needs to make sense out of and to integrate deeper inner
experiences taking place at the core of one's being into a
meaningful response to life.

In this chapter we are attempting to explore the social world
view undergirding the images and themes of the conversion
visions. This chapter will also provide the basis for understanding how values are transmitted through families, caring
others, the church, and culture. These values, ideas, and
symbols legitimate the interpretation that individuals give to
religious experience and the role of the community in these
experiences. Legitimation refers to the structures that provide
meaning to every behavior within a given sphere of influence.
Thus, the task is to spell out in detail the foundational

conceptual and image system that helped slaves and ex-slaves interpret their religious experiences.

The values explored here are also the stuff of which the theological interpretations are made. These values then form the basis of the ability of a community to engage in a hermeneutical process.

In the slave conversion tradition, the deep inner experiences were generally of a revolutionary nature and involved meeting God. Encountering God at the depth of the person's being was the beginning of a process of integrating and interpreting the encounter into a meaningful response. To make a meaningful response, the depth encounter had to be understood in the light of a dynamic thought framework through which all of the person's experiences had to be integrated and interpreted. The very nature of the divine encounter demanded that no area of the person's thought processes and behavior be left untouched. Thus, the encounter precipitated a reinterpretation of life and the world from a new and different perspective, one which would help the experiencer grow into a new and different understanding of himself or herself, others, and the world.

Black persons in and out of slavery lived in a specific symbolic environment. This environment contained several idea or thought symbol systems that influenced the thinking, feelings, and behavior of those who interacted in that environment. Thus, persons undergoing a religious experience could draw on their social world view for help in interpreting and integrating the encounter with God into a meaningful response to life.

The idea system one uses to understand and interpret the encounter with God is called a world view. The world view is an implicit or explicit system of values, beliefs, attitudes, and expectations that influence the behavior of persons. It helps the person find his or her place in life, orders life in meaningful ways, and provides communication among people. It is a socially shared system developed by persons who have interacted with one another over a long period of time. It assists persons to find their place in life and points out what is valuable and what makes life worth living. Moreover, the world view becomes a central factor in helping persons reach growth goals because it points to directions for growth.

The world view revealed in the conversion experiences was Christian and reflected a world where God was still active through Jesus Christ. The world view also showed a shift in the person's way of viewing reality. That is to say, there was a definite shift from a secular, mundane world view to a view of reality that included a transcendent, supernatural dimension. There was also a change in loyalties and commitments by the person that reflected the shift in the two world views mentioned. There was a shift in life-style, commitments, attitudes, behavior, and service. The guidance for these changes came from the Christian world view that existed in the cultural environment.

This chapter is designed to examine the nature of the Christian world view that is evident in the conversion vision reports. The concern is not with the community processes that facilitated the integration and interpretation of the experience into a meaningful response. Rather, our concern is to outline the nature of the contents of the world view.

A world view describes the nature of the world as an orderly system, the nature of human hope within and beyond the world, and the nature of God and human striving for wholeness. This chapter will explore what the conversion visions revealed about these three areas as a way to envision how black persons in and out of slavery sought to respond to their need to make sense out of the world in the light of their new experience.

The significance of the world view is that it helped meet the need for right thinking by persons in a hostile world. Right thinking refers to a way of viewing reality when brokenness and oppression seem to dominate.

All issues regarding the world view will be inferred from the conversion experiences and the biographies. The influences are implied but not explicit in the material.

The Nature of the Cosmos

Two Interpenetrating Realities

It is clear that many persons experiencing the encounter vision had confined their view of the world to the reality of sensual, sensate, and materialistic values before the encounter. They pursued pleasure in sensate form. However, the conversion encounter exposed them to a world beyond the physical, sensate pursuit of pleasure. This "beyond world" was a spiritual world of nonmaterial values, of eternal community, of acceptance and affirmation, as well as a world containing divine spiritual resources. However, this world was not divorced from or antagonistic to the material world in a dualistic sense. Rather, the spiritual world transcended that material, sensate world, but it had an impact on and interacted with the material, sensate world in important ways. The spiritual, transcendent world became immanent or indwelling in the sensate, material world and influenced life's processes and gave meaning and significance to them. The transcendent, spiritual realm opened up the awareness of the experiencer to possibilities, options, and potential for a new life and wholeness that could not be envisaged while one confined one's life to the sensate and materialistic. In short, the cosmos was made up of two interpenetrating and interacting dimensions.

Sojourner Truth provides a prime example of the tension between the material and spiritual world views. Prior to her escape from slavery by her own efforts, she acted on the transcendent and eternal value of freedom at work in the depths of her soul. However, she had not become fully aware of her internal, yet beyond world, which propelled her into freedom. Thus, when she achieved freedom, the old world that she left (Egypt) still had a real claim on her life. She really desired a new life of freedom, but she had not fully relinquished allegiance to her old life, and had not become aware of her need to embrace a new, deeper, broader perspective on life. The spiritual, transcendent world existed while the material, sensate, and physically pleasurable world demanded the dominant place in her life. However, deep in the stirrings of her soul, the spiritual, transcendent dimension of her personality was emerging and demanding her attention. The following example is instructive.

She felt the festival coming. It must have been Whitsuntide. She said she "looked back into Egypt, and everything looked pleasant there." She thought of her companions enjoying the little freedom they had at that moment. She thought of the carnival atmosphere and longed to be back in slavery with her friends. She contrasted this gay time in slavery with the quiet peaceful life she was living in freedom. It seemed tame and unexciting. Her desire to return to slavery was heightened because of her contemplation of enjoying the festivities that accompanied a life of slavery.

She approached one of her friends about returning to slavery. She was advised not to do it because she would only run away again to freedom. She did not listen and attempted to return to slavery by slipping into a wagon heading for her old master's home. It was at this point that a vision appeared to her.

God appeared to her with the suddenness of a flash of lightning and pervaded the universe. There was no place that God was not. She became immediately aware of her "almighty Friend and ever-present help in the time of trouble." Her unfaithfulness appeared before her, and she wanted to hide herself in the bowels of the earth in order "to escape his dreadful presence." She knew there was no place for her to flee.

There was a dread of annihilation which seized her. She felt like she would be swallowed up like "fire licketh up the oil with which it comes in contact." She felt unworthy to speak and desired someone to speak for her. She wanted someone worthy in the sight of heaven to speak for her. A friend did appear to stand between her and God. She desired to know who this friend was. She asked who this friend was, and the vision brightened into a distinct form beaming with love.

When she didn't recognize the visitant, the visitant became restless. Then, the insight came to her that this friend was Jesus. Jesus confirmed this. She then proclaimed she knew Jesus in a personal way. She knew him as someone who loved her and that always loved her. Her heart was full of joy and gladness. She no longer wanted to return to slavery.[1]

Sojourner became aware of the spiritual dimension in her life when she decided to exchange freedom for bondage. She said she looked back into Egypt. She plotted her return to slavery. She had what the apostle Paul would call the spirit of slavery (Rom. 8:15). Yet, God's claim on her life through the spiritual dimension brought forcefully to her awareness the insaneness of her regressive decision. Thus, the spiritual realm interrupted the normal thought processes going on in Sojourner's mind, and showed her the growth-blocking and faulty dimension of her thought. Her logic was not logical: If I go back into slavery, I will be a happy slave. However, the right thinking produced by the vision encounter was, If I accept my freedom, I will be a responsible, authentic person fully in charge of my own life, gaining happiness through a meaningful life of self-giving.

Right thinking, then, for Sojourner, involved grasping God's relationship to her and viewing all dimensions of her life in the light of that relationship. For her, God was at the center of life. Thus, living the life of responsible freedom was possible because God was a dynamic force generating power for her to become a free and whole person. To seek her fulfillment in a Saturday-night social was not only idolatrous thinking, it was also growth-blocking thinking. It would not produce wholeness.

Sojourner's encounter with God reveals a view of the world having two interpenetrating dimensions. The spiritual dimension could have a life-transforming impact on the material reality.

Open or Closed System

Closely related to the cosmological view of the world as an interpenetration of nonmaterial and material realities is the view of the universe as an open system. The view of the world as a closed mechanical system of cause-and-effect laws has been the dominant view expressed by science until recently. In the closed-system view of the world, reality is portrayed as one-dimensional. There is no intervention by a nonmaterial world.

An open-system view of reality, on the other hand, takes full cognizance that there is a natural as well as a spiritual realm. However, the natural realm is not closed but is open to influences from the spiritual realm. This open-system view was the view of persons in and out of bondage. They expected help from God in their mundane existence in life. They did not limit their view of reality to one dimension.

The case of Sojourner Truth revealed this open-systems view. The material world was opened to influences from the spiritual realm. On her behalf God intervened via a revelatory vision to make her aware of the growth-reversing decision she was making to return to slavery. Evidently, her thought to return to slavery had a self-hatred side to it, and she needed to experience divine love in order to do something worthwhile for herself. Thus, the supernatural depth dimension of love penetrated the boundaries of the material world and bestowed on her worth. The spiritual resources of the immaterial world were made available to the material world. This open-systems view was also true in the experiences of many other slaves.

J. W. C. Pennington and Harriet Tubman both believed that prayer could influence God to bring spiritual resources to bear on the conditions that black people faced in slavery. For example, Pennington felt that prayer was instrumental in eliciting God's aid on behalf of those oppressed and scarred by slavery. Commenting on God's action resulting from sincere prayer, Pennington says:

But I am not the less confident that sincere prayer to God, proceeding from a few hearts deeply imbued with experimental Christianity about *that time*, has had much to do with subsequent happy results. At that time the 800,000 bondmen in the British Isles had not seen the beginning of the end of their sufferings—at that time, 20,000 who are now free in Canada, were in bonds—at that time, there was no Vigilance Committee to aid the flying slave—at that time, the two powerful Anti-Slavery Societies of America had no being.[2]

Obviously, he felt that earnest prayer by sincere people assisted in helping God to make the decision to use supernatural resources to speed up the freedom process. It was spiritual resources working with human potential that helped to bring changes in slavery, in the minds of many.

Right thinking involved how the person in and out of bondage saw the spiritual and physical worlds. The one-dimensional, social, and human world did not have the last word. No, rather it was the existence of the spiritual world and its impact in the physical, material world that assisted the person in slavery to gain the right perspective on life and suffering. Right thinking involved, then, recognizing the resources existing beyond the material world.

Relationship of Body and Soul

If the natural world is a closed system and if there is no interpenetration between the natural world and the spiritual world, then the relationship of the body and the soul is confined to a naturalistic understanding. Thus, the word *spirit* is often substituted for the word *soul*, and the spirit within the natural realm is one-dimensional. Any relationship of soul to the nonmaterial world is often dismissed as Gnostic. Gnostic dualism perceived the soul as a prisoner of the body and therefore needing to be freed from the body.[3] Contrasting this was a belief by those in slavery that the soul was not imprisoned in the body or by social conditions. Rather, the soul and body are intricately related, but the resources of the spiritual world were made available to persons through that part of the human self called the soul. The soul, then, was that aspect of the self that helped the person relate to God and to the spiritual resources for transcending as well as for fighting oppression.

The saving of the soul was important to black people in and out of slavery. But as far as we can tell, the saving was from false loyalty, idolatry, and hell, not from an imprisonment in the body. The concern was to liberate the soul from false bondage to an idolatrous world view and hell. Thus, to have one's soul freed meant to experience the assurance of one's salvation through a conversion experience, but it also meant changing the way one lived.

One respondent interviewed for the Fisk University study said, "I claim that unless one has heard God's voice—felt his love—in other words, unless one has had his soul freed from hell in such a way that he knows it, one would remain a sinner, and in heaven there is no room for a sinner."[4]

This quotation seems to point to a duality between this life and heaven, where this world is rejected. However, the person reporting talks about a following of a dynamic inner voice which leads her in living a life of commitment to others and living as an example. Thus, the soul and the way one lived in the body were related. The soul became the new center of a person's life, and this new center helped to organize all of life around itself. Thus, the body was affected by what happened to the soul.

Right thinking in regard to body and soul helped one to see the limits of confining one's center to the body and its pleasures. However, to have one's soul saved did not mean divorcing the soul from the body. Rather, it brought the body under the new center's influence. This, indeed, would lead to meaning and wholeness. Encountering God led to a renewed body and a commitment to participation in life. In fact, the narrative reveals a deep commitment to life by those who had met God face to face.[5]

Indeed, the language of the conversion experience seems Gnostic in that the body and soul are envisioned as split with the body as the temple and the soul occupying a space which the soul vacates at death and returns to God.[6] Yet, to impose a Gnostic world view on these ideas is to miss the holism undergirding the lived life of the black person in bondage. The assumption here is that right thinking is reflected in the lived life. Therefore, a person with a saved soul who lives a full life of participation reflects an implicit world view of holism where body and soul are intricately related.

Ideas have a context. When the conversion ideas expressed are placed in a context of lived life, what emerges is an implicit world view undergirding an explicit view of life. This implicit world view is reflected in the behavior of persons as full participants in life and points to a holism. This holism envisages an interpenetration that is natural and supernatural, an open-system view of the natural world, and the intimate relationship of the body and soul.

The Nature of Hope

The assurances of the soul's salvation and that a person was going to heaven were revealed through the conversion experience. The explicit thinking of persons in and out of bondage revealed concern for assurance of one's election by God to receive eternal life in the future.[7] Yet, this assurance of future salvation was something that had to be experienced in the present. Thus, one's election by God was revealed in the present by the conversion vision. Listen to one respondent:

> How can we find God? God has a chosen people. He has always had a chosen people, and he calls whomsoever he wills. Any child who has been born of the spirit knows it, for he has felt God's power, tasted his love, and seen the travel of his own soul.[8]

Again the distinction between expressed words and lived experience is the key for the interpretation of the implicit world view. What was central in the implicit world view was a realized experience of the hope that was to come in the future. Thus, there was a "now" dimension to the hope. It can be said that hope for the person in bondage was present, realized, and proleptic. That is to say, hope was experienced as a present realized reality. Moreover, the future expectation of salvation was proleptic in that the future was lived as if it were a present reality.[9]

In each of the conversion experiences analyzed for this manuscript the future reality of wholeness, peace, justice, and perfect love was experienced as a present reality because they existed in the spiritual and nonmaterial realm as a reality and became actualized possibilities in the world of lived experience. When one's life was in harmony with the spiritual reality, the resources of that spiritual reality were experienced just as if they were fully actualized in mundane reality. Thus, the slaves were not escapists seeking the compensatory rewards of heaven because of the poverty and barrenness of their present reality. Rather, they tapped into a reservoir of existing hope that energized them for full participation in the present.

The realized eschatological hope and the attention paid to the assurance of the soul's salvation represented the influence of Puritan ideas on the slave culture. Sixteenth-century Puritanism was concerned to pacify the conscience of persons preoccupied with the soul's eternal damnation in hell, and, therefore, people sought assurance that they were saved.[10] To assume that the black person in bondage was motivated by the same Puritan preoccupation with avoiding eternal damnation, however, is to fall into a grave error. The black person in bondage used the images, symbols, and word forms employed by the wider community to express his or her ideas, but the underlying motivation was different. The doctrine of election and the assurance of salvation and liberation were not only related to the soul's destiny, but also to the hope for peace, justice, wholeness, and humaneness in the present. These Puritan doctrines differed from the original Calvinistic conceptions. The form was the same, but the content, experience, and historical context differed.

The realized proleptic nature of the black Christian experience was not confined to the narratives compiled for this study. The theme of realized proleptic eschatology can be found in the writings of such historical black persons as Nathaniel Paul (1755–1839), Richard Allen (1760–1831), and James W. C. Pennington (1812–1871).[11]

Realized proleptic eschatology was present along with a future eschatology in the writings of black people from that period.[12] Yet, this eschatological orientation related to the hope for physical as well as spiritual liberation. There was a concern for the coming of the kingdom of God as a living reality within the historical process.[13] Thus, the worldly concerns for freedom and the experience of God's presence in the depths of their being made the future a present reality which would be actualized fully later in history.

Right thinking in the midst of oppression involved interpreting the movement of God at the core of one's being in ways that facilitated growth. Focusing on a postponed future would have been, indeed, escapist. But a realized future enabled full participation.

African and Biblical Background of Eschatological World View

There are two sources of influence for understanding the realized eschatological view of black people in and out of slavery. These sources are biblical eschatology and African eschatology.

Albert Raboteau has pointed out that the images appearing in the slave conversion encounters closely resemble those images recorded in the book of Revelation.[14] This, then, raises the question of the relatedness of apocalyptic literature and eschatology of the New Testament and the book of Daniel in the Old Testament to the conversion encounters of black people in and out of bondage.

Prior to exploring the relationship of the conversion encounters of black people to apocalyptic literature, it is important to explore the African eschatology through John S. Mbiti's book, *New Testament Eschatology in African Background.*

The key issue related by Mbiti is the importance of the two-dimensional orientation to time when compared to the three-dimensional view of time.[15] The two-dimensional orientation toward time emphasizes the past and the present with little emphasis on the future. The three-dimensional view of time focuses on the past, present, and indefinite future. Whether one focuses on a two- or three-dimensional view of time, how time is visualized influences one's orientation toward biblical time. For example, the western view of time is three-dimensional, and therefore there is an emphasis on future eschatology when examining the biblical record. The African, on the other hand, views future time in terms of a definite time in the near future of six months to two years. Thus, realized eschatology in the biblical record would get more emphasis in African thinking.

103

Given the African time heritage of a two-dimensional view of time, the realized eschatology of black people in and out of bondage is understandable. The time heritage, then, helps to provide a link to the cultural basis for proleptic eschatology in the black Christian experience. This two-dimensional orientation of black Christians also helps to give focus to the relationship of apocalyptic literature to the conversion tradition of black persons in and out of slavery.

There are common features in the literary genre called apocalypse. These are (1) a concept of angels and demons, (2) the idea of two ages, (3) depiction of the end of an age, (4) rich symbolism and imagery, (5) pessimism and determinism, and a doctrine of life after death.[16]

Paul Hanson elaborates the apocalyptic genre. His description of the apocalyptic genre includes (1) a revelation from God, (2) through a mediator such as Jesus Christ or a messenger such as an angel, (3) to a seer, (4) concerning future events.[17] Often this revelation would come in a vision where a person is able to peer into the spiritual realm to see future events. Moreover, the interpretation of the event comes from an angel, and this angel often becomes a guide through heavenly places. The vision often turns to rapture and is followed by a word of comfort.

We examine the following encounter vision report for its apocalyptic features.

There is a case of a man who heard a voice while plowing in a field. He was afraid, and dropped his plow. However, a voice of comfort came and told him not to be afraid. The sky grew dark, and he fell to the ground. A vision of a new world appeared, and a voice cried out, "I am blessed, but you are damned."

An angel appeared to him and touched him. He said he looked new. His feet and hands were new. He said, "I looked and saw my old body suspended over a burning pit by a small web like a spider web." Then he heard a voice that said, "I have loved you with an everlasting love. You are this day made alive and freed from hell. You are a chosen vessel unto the Lord. Be upright before me, and I will guide you unto all truth. My grace is sufficient for you. Go, and I am with you. Preach the gospel, and I will preach with you. You are henceforth the salt of the earth."[18]

In the above case an angel of the Lord was apparent. The vision pictures a new world in the midst of darkness and fear. He was witnessing the future end of the world. A voice comforted him, and he was changed in the process. He could observe his old self hung over a pit, but he was a new person with new hands and feet. While the new world had not come, his changed life had eventuated.

There is no doubt that this comes close to the apocalyptic genre. Similarities include a concept of angels and demons, rich symbolism and imagery, a revelation from God through an angel, and a vision of a new age to come. This conclusion is further supported in that this apocalyptic vision occurred in a time of oppression and functioned to comfort and bring life in spite of oppression.[19] It brought God's supernatural resources to bear on the person's need. In other words, the source of the vision was a vehicle of divine resources for the black person in bondage.

As indicated earlier, the African background of slave eschatology was the immediate future rather than the indefinite future. Thus, the content of the vision of black people in and out of bondage was realized eschatology. The resources of the supernatural were brought to bear on the present life of the person, and the person experienced the future as if it were already a completed reality. Thus, the content of the above apocalyptic vision reflected realized eschatology in that the person experienced new life in his present life.

This realized eschatology is different from the future eschatology in Daniel and Revelation. There is no postponing of the victory over evil as in Daniel or Revelation. Even the new world of the future was experienced as if it were realized. Other than this difference in eschatological outlook, the genre or form and structure of the above slave vision and apocalyptic vision in Scripture are similar. This, then, bespeaks of a universal form manifesting itself in the lives of people at a time of personal, physical, and social oppression. In a real way, though, the apocalyptic content of the black conversion vision reflected the realized eschatology present in other positions of the New Testament such as the Gospel of John.[20]

The brief excursion into the African and biblical basis of black realized eschatology has been intended to point out its distinctive quality. The structure, form, and content of the realized eschatological vision was thoroughly biblical as well as historical, social, and cultural. Its origin reflected biblical influence as well as the oppressive social circumstances and the African cultural contexts.

The Nature of God

The relationship between God and the black person in and out of bondage was one created and initiated by God. The black person encountering God saw the encounter as ordained by God, and the person, then, saw himself or herself as sought out rather than forsaken in a land of bondage. Thus, God was immanently involved in the daily affairs of people and in community.

God was incarnate in Jesus Christ, who encountered persons daily. The cosmological resources of the transcendent world of reality became resources for the person in bondage, and suffering oppression became concretized in the person's life in the encounter. Thus, God's work through Jesus enabled the black person to participate in the actualized future in the present. The encounter with God in Jesus Christ facilitated liberation from personal and physical bondage, met certain spiritual and psychological needs, and brought meaning and significance to chaotic inner turmoil.

God's capacity for relationship and for being present in the lives of persons was significant in the conversion encounters. The conversion encounter affirmed the person's worth and self-esteem, and thus, God was viewed as a person capable of being in relationship. In relationship, God's person and action are merged. Thus, God's person and God's work were experienced in theophany—encounter with God.

God's capacity for relationship and the black person's encountering God in relationship led black Christians to put emphasis on the experience of God as determinative of one's Christian identity. One had to experience God's love directly, and this experience became the certification of one's true identity as a child of God. Thus, through experience one encountered the true nature of God through Jesus Christ. A child of God was one who was born of the spirit and whose soul had been saved from hell.

The incarnated God of the slaves and ex-slaves was not a God of radical immanence where God was divested of the divine and transcendent identity. The incarnated God still was the transcendent, supernatural God who brought about wholeness naturally and supernaturally. Thus, the incarnation was a paradox of the presence of the immanent and transcendent dimensions of God.

The Social Psychology of Conversion

The social psychology of conversion refers to the analysis of critical issues related to the world view undergirding the slave conversion tradition.

Two critical academic issues are raised by this chapter. First, is conversion a private, static, and once-and-for-all event which is divorced from cultural context and symbolic world views?[21] Second, is the person predisposed to impose religious meanings on significant inner changes that have taken place?[22]

To address the first issue, conversion is not divorced from the social context. Indeed, the ability to describe in detail the events of the encounter presupposed an existing language and symbol system capable of making sense out of the encounter or experience. Biblical imagery and African symbolism provided interpretive tools for the experiencer of conversion. Although the conversion encounter was private, it was by no means static or divorced from context. The precise nature of the social context and its function before and after the conversion encounter is the subject of the next chapter.

The second issue relates to whether or not the person experiencing the conversion encounter was predisposed to impose a religious interpretation on that conversion event. The answer is affirmative here. The context in which the slaves and ex-slaves lived predisposed them to apply religious meaning to significant inner happenings. Biblical stories and images as well as their African religious heritages permeated the slave environment. The only other alternative symbol systems existing in slavery and its aftermath to interpret their experiences of God were superstition and magic, which they distinguished from true Christianity. Secular interpretations did not seem viable. Indeed, the inner changes were the result of the supernatural intervention of God.

Right thinking was crucial for the black person. The experience was central, but how one understood the experience so it produced wholeness required right thinking. The symbolic world view provided the tools for right thinking and enabled the person to make a meaningful response.

The world view had an impact on the way people interpreted their experiences. Thus, the social psychology of conversion relates directly to the role of culture in hermeneutics. This concern is raised in the next section.

Hermeneutical Concerns

The liberating work of God freed persons from the false and idolatrous views that blocked a person's growth. This was true in the case of Sojourner Truth. She felt that the fun and gaiety of festivals were better than the boredom and responsibility of freedom. Her faulty thought system was leading her back into slavery and into regressed growth. Her ideas became idolatrous in that they became norms around which she evaluated her life in freedom. True freedom is having the kind of idea system that makes God's liberating activity the norm or the center of one's life. With God's liberating activity as the center freeing people to grow toward meaning, there is no thought of exchanging one's real freedom for bondage of any kind—economic, social, emotional, intellectual, or spiritual. It is only when a substitute idea becomes the center around which everything else is organized that bondage takes place.

In the hermeneutics of engagement the first step is the discernment of God's central activity in the past. It also involves the discernment of the central image or concepts that are used to express this activity. This chapter has revealed that there were concepts—the cosmos as two interpenetrating realities, the universe as an open system, the interrelatedness of the body and the soul, realized eschatology, and the apocalyptic genre of the slave encounter visions—that accompany the liberating-growth-meaning action of God. It has been discovered in this study that God's liberating activity took place, but it also had to be interpreted. The slaves' and ex-slaves' world view and image system provided them with a way to apprehend what God was doing through an intricate theological and philosophical system. They were able to envisage God's action in their lives in holistic ways rather than in compartmentalized ways.

It must be added here that the manner in which the slaves and ex-slaves apprehended the world with God's central activity in it is similar to the epistemology in modern process philosophical thinking. Moreover, the emphasis on holism and open systems is akin to modern systems thinking in behavioral science. However, it must also be pointed out that the slave and ex-slave world views were not systematic process theologies. They were rooted in supernaturalism, realized eschatology, and biblical images. Ex-slaves and slaves did not emphasize radical immanence at the expense of supernatural transcendence. Both were present. It could be concluded that the slave's and ex-slaves' view of the world was a supernatural-transcendent-immanent-biblical-growth-hope-wholeness model.

The hermeneutical process used by the slaves to interpret their encounter with God is important. One way to look at the interpretation and reinterpretation process is to examine the impact the conversion visions had on the existing thought system of the slave. Were there transitions in the thought systems of the slaves and ex-slaves because of conversion?

The answer is yes. That is, there was a shift from a self-centered world to a spiritual world. However, this spiritual centering was accompanied by a synthesis of the spiritual and material rather than a dichotomizing of them.

What can be seen in the hermeneutics of the slaves following conversion was an expanding of the slaves' world view. Life included a dynamic which freed all life from bondage. They developed discernment that went beyond sensate vision, and they could actually see God at work bringing about the liberation of the whole person. The slaves' spiritual vision improved. They could not only visualize the interrelatedness of the world, but they could discern where God was carrying out God's liberating activity.

The hermeneutical process used by slaves and ex-slaves to derive meaning from events can be evaluated in Fowler's model in *Stages of Faith*. While there will be no effort to show a transition from Stage 4 to Stage 5 in Fowler's system, there is an effort to show a transition from an exclusively material, social world view to a spiritual-wholeness world view that is characteristic of Fowler's Stage 5. Fowler's Stage 4 seems characteristic of college- and university-trained people of today, so it is inadequate for the description of the slave world view. However, Stage 5 seems characteristic of the slave Christian world view.

There appears to be a movement from a one-dimensional view of reality by the slave and ex-slave to a bidimensional view of reality. One-dimensional views of reality focus on the sensate, the material, and the pursuit of pleasure, without much attention to the transcendent and the spiritual. However, the transition to a more inclusive world view included a view of the world as interrelated, open, where opposites are united, and the body and soul were related. Thus, the fifth stage of the slave and ex-slave world view represented a completion of a fractured world view.

This chapter on the psychosocial nature of the hermeneutical process has lifted up the social nature of hermeneutics without giving much attention to the psychological or intrapersonal dimension of hermeneutics. The question is, how are they related?

In the last chapter, we talked about the hermeneutics of the unconscious where the interpretation and reinterpretation process took place outside of the awareness of the person. Yet, how is the hermeneutics of the unconscious related to the world view hermeneutics of this chapter? We emphasize that they work together. However, when adequate social symbols for interpreting reality do not exist, the hermeneutics of the unconscious is more prevalent in the life of the person. Thus, God's revelation is not totally dependent on social symbols existing in the cultural environment. Cultural symbols can be carried as part of the collective unconscious or as inherited dimensions of collective history not available to the conscious mind. Yet when tradition is inadequate for transmitting symbols and images, they then find their way into our lives primarily through dreams. However, when social tradition is adequate for transmitting symbols and images, the collective unconscious keeps tradition alive by continually legitimizing and reinforcing the images, symbols, and concepts. That is, the collective unconscious reinforces cultural images, symbols, and ideas and helps to draw people to them.

In the next chapter more will be said about how cultural symbols and images are part of the interpretation and reinterpretation process. Here we have pointed to the nature of symbols, image, and concepts which relate to God's activity in the liberation-growth-meaning process. In the next we will examine the communal dimension of the interpretation-reinterpretation process.

Notes

1. Sojourner Truth, *Narrative of Sojourner Truth* (Boston: J. B. Yerrington & Son, 1850), pp. 64-68.
2. James W. C. Pennington, "The Fugitive Blacksmith" (London: Charles Gilpin, 1849), published in *The American Negro: History and Literature* (New York: Arno Press and the New York Times, 1968), p. 52.

3. For a discussion of Gnostic dualism, see Morton Kelsey, *Healing and Christianity: In Ancient Thought and Modern Times* (New York: Harper & Row, 1973), p. 49.

4. Clifton H. Johnson, *God Struck Me Dead*, p. 101.

5. Ibid., pp. vii-xii. See the foreword written by Paul Radin.

6. Ibid., p. 14.

7. Ibid., pp. 13-14.

8. Ibid., p. 13.

9. Edward P. Wimberly, "Contributions of Black Christians to the Discipline of Pastoral Care," *Reflection* 80 (January 1983): 4-8.

10. Brooks E. Holifield, *A History of Pastoral Care in America: From Salvation to Self-Realization* (Nashville: Abingdon Press, 1983), pp. 23-25.

11. See Henry J. Young, *Major Black Religious Leaders 1755-1940* (Nashville: Abingdon Press, 1977).

12. Ibid., p. 34.

13. Ibid., p. 14.

14. Albert J. Raboteau, *Slave Religion: The "Invisible Institution" in the Antebellum South* (New York: Oxford University Press, 1978), p. 269.

15. John S. Mbiti, *New Testament Eschatology in an African Background* (London: Oxford University Press, 1971), pp. 40-60.

16. James M. Efird, *Daniel and Revelation: A Study of Two Extraordinary Visions* (Valley Forge: Judson Press, 1978), pp. 11-17.

17. Paul Hanson, "Apocalypticism," *The Interpreter's Dictionary of the Bible: Supplementary Volume* (Nashville: Abingdon Press, 1976), pp. 27-28.

18. Johnson, *God Struck Me Dead*, pp. 15-18.

19. Ibid., p. 27; Efird, *Daniel and Revelation*, p. 8; George W. E. Nickelsburg, *Jewish Literature Between the Bible and the Mishnah* (Philadelphia: Fortress Press, 1981), p. 1; and Michael E. Stone, *Scriptures, Sects and Visions* (Philadelphia: Fortress Press, 1980), p. 62. All point out that oppression was the context of apocalyptic literature.

20. Gayraud S. Wilmore, *Last Things First* (Philadelphia: Westminster Press, 1982), pp. 77-96. Wilmore makes the same conclusion about realized eschatology in black Christianity.

21. Cedric B. Johnson and Newton H. Malony, *Christian Conversion: Biblical and Psychological Perspectives* (Grand Rapids: Zondervan, 1982), p. 22.

22. Ibid., p. 25. They refer to the psychological predisposition of persons prior to contact with the new universe of meaning.

Chapter 7

THE IMPLICATIONS OF THE SLAVE CONVERSION TRADITION FOR A POSTMODERN AGE

The problem that faces any contemporary community of faith is the recovery of a meaningful faith. The basic problem is translating the central dynamic of God's activity revealed in its tradition into meaningful symbols that communicate in the present. This has been the central hermeneutical task facing each faith community generation throughout the history of the church, and it is our task now.

Four contemporary hermeneutical approaches can be discerned that relate the central dynamic of its faith tradition to the community today. These methods include supernaturalism, naturalism, existentialism, and cultural theology.

Supernaturalism has attempted to use the categories and symbols created by today's industrial, technological society to defend itself and to communicate its message, according to Paul Tillich.[1] In this approach, supernaturalists have drawn on their traditional past in doctrine, cult, and message; but they contradict the message by using categories created by the industrial spirit against which they are fighting. Harvey Cox echoes this same critique of supernaturalism by pointing to the use of multimedia by many fundamentalist groups.[2]

Naturalism in Christian theology has attempted to interpret the central message of the gospel for today by accepting the new situation caused by the industrial, technological society.

They have accepted the new situation by adapting and appropriating the gospel message in contemporary symbols. This gave birth to liberal theology, and Tillich points out that liberal theology paid the price of adaptation by losing the central message of the faith.[3]

An alternative to supernaturalism and naturalism is existential theology, with which Tillich is identified. He says that historical providence opened another avenue for relating religion to twentieth-century Western culture, and this alternative is existentialism.[4] Existentialism as a philosophy emerged as a protest against the reducing of people to objects in industrial, technological society. Because this society treats human beings as means toward ends, humanity's existential predicament is the experience of emptiness, meaninglessness, dehumanization, and estrangement. Tillich's hermeneutics, then, correlates questions raised by existential analysis of the human predicament with the message of the Christian gospel. Existential analysis raises questions that Christian theology then answers.

The fourth alternative is cultural theology, or story theology, represented by Harvey Cox. What distinguishes Cox's method of culture theology from Tillich's theology of culture is that Cox is writing in what he calls a postmodern phase of theology while Tillich wrote in the phase of modernity. For Cox, the postmodern age is characterized by inversions.[5] Since Schleiermacher, theology has chosen the emerging intellectual life of the community to do its hermeneutical dialogue. This was the case with Tillich; he aimed his writing toward existential philosophical movements. However, postmodern theology reverses this way of doing theology and focuses on the needs of the disinherited and culturally dominated rather than on the critics or culture despisers of religion that dominate the intellectual life of modern society. Thus, for Cox, the emerging hermeneutics in theology must find ways to dialogue with those on the periphery and at the bottom. For him, the challenge is the hermeneutics of folk religion and grass-roots piety.

Indeed, theological hermeneutics has changed in the postmodern period; and folk religion and biblical faith, with their supernatural-naturalistic world view, will become sources of contemporary theology because of their ability to respond to the needs of those who have become disenchanted with the promises of modernity. Yet, how we draw on past folk religion, present folk religion, and biblical faith in the light of postmodern society is still the basic hermeneutical question. This task will be explored in this final chapter by taking hermeneutical clues from the slave and ex-slave tradition and correlating it with the hermeneutics of engagement espoused by Paul Hanson. Our concern is to develop a hermeneutical model useful for the church in general which brings the past to bear on the present in ways that continue God's liberation of human wholeness. It is also our attempt to link God's immanence and transcendence in the model. Case studies and critical issues, such as the relationship of science and theology and the place of hermeneutics in ministry, will be explored within the proposed hermeneutical model.

A Hermeneutical Model

The hermeneutical model for linking the past and present to interpret and reinterpret contemporary experience is the hermeneutics of engagement. By way of summary, the hermeneutics of engagement has three basic steps.[6] Step one involves discerning the central dynamic of faith embodied in tradition through responsible historical critical study. Step two involves living within a faith community that has committed itself to the central dynamic of faith revealed in tradition. It is this faith community that carries out the critical examination of the past. Step three assists the central dynamic of faith revealed in tradition by engaging the events and issues of the contemporary world. Each of these steps will be examined in detail. This skeletal outline will be filled in with the content discovered in examining the slave and ex-slave narrative tradition and with contemporary issues confronting the church as a whole. The parameters of the model will be contained in these three steps proposed by Hanson.

Discernment of God's Activity in the Slave and Ex-slave Community

This step assumes that any contemporary faith community derives its identity from dialogue with its heritage of faith and mission. Therefore, examining the faith tradition and its development over time is an essential step in hermeneutics. Because the contemporary world and the worlds comprising the faith heritage are different, this first step allows the contemporary faith community to discern what has been consistent throughout the heritage.

For our purposes, the heritage to which we are referring is the Christian heritage of black people in America which is rooted in Scripture, related to its African heritage, and developed as a result of God's involvement in the community. This faith heritage began in slavery and has continued to the present day. Thus, knowing what has remained dynamically consistent within this heritage is essential for the interpretation and reinterpretation process today. Moreover, such an approach can reveal general guidelines and parameters that can be utilized in postmodern theology.

An essential problem emerges when a faith community attempts to understand its heritage. This problem is whether what is discerned in tradition is inferred through the critical analytical powers of the mind, or whether it is caught or apprehended by the whole person because of its dynamic and living character. This problem is raised by existential theology, which posits that the central universal, dynamic, and unconditional facet of a faith heritage is not inferred analytically, but is apprehended immediately.[7] Our position is that the awareness of the central dynamic of faith in tradition is revealed as one becomes involved in the contemporary faith community as well as participates in the heritage that gave birth to the faith community. Thus, understanding and discerning are apprehended and caught but not inferred. Yet, analytical reason and inferential abilities are needed when the immediate awareness of the central dynamic of faith has to be recorded systematically. Inference is needed when what is caught has to be translated, developed, and related to other

116

areas of life. Moreover, technical reason is needed when what is caught is abstracted from its context and related to another context. Thus, experiential catching and intuitive knowing must work hand in hand with inferential knowing.

The central dynamic of faith revealed in the study of the black Christian heritage has been the liberating activity of God that brings about human wholeness in mind, body, spirit, and in relationship to others, society, and institutions. What was caught was that God is alive, incarnated, and working through natural and supernatural means to bring about human wholeness. What has been inferred rationally is how this alive, central dynamic of faith relates to spiritual, psychological, psychosocial, community, and cultural needs.

We have inferred from our heritage six basic levels of God's liberating activity that bring about human wholeness. They are (1) liberation from personal sin and guilt; (2) liberation from social, economic, material, and political oppression; (3) liberation from developmental, transitional, and situational psychological crises and stresses that have the potential for blocking growth; (4) liberation psychosocially of persons from penultimate, proximate, and finite world views that block growth toward wholeness; (5) liberation of community and interpersonal relationships to facilitate growth; and (6) liberation through cultural mediums such as ritual to help the community organize its activity around holistic and liberating values.

Our inferred conclusion is that our immediate awareness of God as liberator has many levels. This is qualified by the knowledge that where God is at work today is discerned and caught rather than inferred, and therefore, our cooperation with God may lead us to one level of liberation or another. Because of the domination of inferential analysis in liberal theological and ministerial settings, some of our preference for either social activism or personal ministry has been generated by our inferential analysis rather than from a prayerful discernment of where God is actually carrying out liberating activity. Inferential awareness operates out of principles, whereas discernment emerges out of an awareness of what

God is doing. However, inferential awareness informs discernment of liberation, and it helps to give shape to a response to God's liberating activity. Discernment without inferential strategies is blind, but inferential strategies without discernment of what God is doing is powerless. Our social action, as well as all of our personal ministries, needs to be rooted in the discernment of where God is at work buttressed by the appropriate inferential strategy.

The first hermeneutical step, then, helps us discern and infer God's central dynamic activity in the faith heritage. God as the liberator of human wholeness is discerned and experienced, but the relationship of this liberating activity to various areas of life is inferred. The implication of the concepts of discernment and inferential awareness is that God encounters the faith community in the present and encountered the faith community in the past in similar ways. This discussion of the relationship between the past and the contemporary faith community brings us to the second step in the hermeneutics of engagement.

Participation in God's Liberating Activity

The second step in the hermeneutics of engagement is commitment to the liberating activity of God in the present community of faith. The liberating activity of God operating in the faith heritage is still active and alive in the present. It is the task of the community of faith to be aware of God's liberating activity and become committed to what God is doing. What God did in the past is incarnated in the present, and by its very nature demands a response through commitment. God's supernatural and natural liberating activity take place in today's communities of faith.

The contemporary community of faith, then, is an extension of the historical and present liberating activity of God. In the Old Testament, God was the liberator of the Children of Israel. In the New Testament and in the slave and ex-slave community, the same liberating activity of God in the Old Testament was accomplished through the person of Jesus Christ and the Holy Spirit. God, Jesus Christ, and the Holy

Spirit were without theoretical distinction for the slaves and ex-slaves because the emphasis seemed to be on God and how Jesus Christ and the Holy Spirit functioned to bring about God's purposes. Today, the liberation of human wholeness is also accomplished by God in the faith community through Jesus Christ and the Holy Spirit. These three Persons are viewed as carrying out the same liberating function. More precisely, the Holy Spirit is viewed as God's presence working liberating activity in the present. Jesus Christ is also viewed in the same way.

Because God's liberating activity is present and continues in the faith community through Jesus Christ and the Holy Spirit, our task is to be committed to and to cooperate with God's liberating activity within our faith community. The first step in commitment and cooperation is to be aware of what God is doing. The second step is to be open to what God is doing, and the third step is to organize the faith community's whole life around the central values and work of God, the liberator. To organize itself around the central liberating activity of God means that the worship, caring, nurturing, and witnessing life of the community must participate in and reflect the liberating work of God.

To illustrate how the faith community can organize its whole life around the liberating acts of God to produce human wholeness, an example can be drawn from the slave tradition. This community was formed by forgiven sinners who had encountered God in a personal way. Because of the love and feelings of worth bestowed by the experience, they sought to respond to God's initiative in love and service to others. This love and service included participation in the ritual life of the community of faith, caring through support structures in the faith community, nurturing the growth of others, witnessing to the liberating acts of God through evangelism, and addressing social structures that hindered holistic growth.

So far, we have explored the faith community's commitment to the central liberating act of God in its life. A central theological task needs to be discussed before continuing this section. This theological task relates to how the community of faith becomes aware of God's activity to liberate holistic growth of persons. Is it caught and apprehended immediately by those who are open to God's work, or is it inferred through reflecting on the faith heritage? This is the same debate raised earlier with regard to the place of experiential ontology in faith (characteristic of Tillich's thinking) and the place of technical, rational processes in faith.

Our answer to this question is that God's liberating activity is caught as one encounters God while he or she participates in the community of faith. One becomes immediately aware of God's existential presence as one encounters God in community. Yet, one's immediate awareness must use technical reason to draw out the implications of the encounter for total participation in community. Holistic growth demands the ability to infer from the immediate awareness of God's encountering presence what this awareness means intrapersonally, interpersonally, spiritually, socially, institutionally, and politically. Thus, intuitive knowing and knowledge through inferral reasoning work hand in hand in the holistic growth process. The study of Scripture and tradition are essential if the community of faith is to be enriched and enabled to assist in the holistic growth of its members. People cannot grow unless they are able to use technical reasoning to plumb the depths of what they have apprehended and encountered immediately in God.

The second step of the hermeneutical process is commitment by the faith community to the liberating act of God. This means that the people must encounter God in their participation in community and use technical reasoning to translate the experience into meaningful responses. That is, the encounter with God has personal, interpersonal, social, institutional, cultural, political, economic, spiritual, and evangelical implications. When the implications of the encounter with God are translated, through the help of Scripture and tradition, into a meaningful interpretive response, hermeneutics or the process of interpretation and reinterpretation has taken place.

Fidelity to Ontology of Events

How the faith community translates the encounter with God into meaningful holistic responses is crucial. Answering the question of "how" brings us to the third stage of hermeneutics of engagement. It is through relating the central liberating activity of God, apprehended personally within the faith community, to the major events taking place in the world that meaningful responses are made. The third step in the hermeneutical process is to cooperate with God in confronting life. The basic assumption here is that God is actively engaging the major events and issues of today, and it is the task of the faith community to apprehend what God is doing and develop strategies for cooperating with God's liberating activity. Thus, the ontology of events—God's engaging present-day events—requires both apprehending abilities and technical reasoning abilities. We need spiritual discernment to apprehend what God is doing today, but we also need to discover through inferential reasoning how best to cooperate with God. Here prayer and study are related.

The major task in the third step of hermeneutics of engagement is the exegesis of culture and prayerfully seek God's revelation concerning where God is at work. With regard to prayerful seeking of God's activity, this means an awareness that certain events within the community have their *kairos* or special time, season, or opportunity where God is actively completing God's purpose. This *kairos* relates to personal liberation and social liberation. Only a community in prayer can discern the *kairos* movement associated with God's activity. Yet, to have an informed strategy for cooperating with God, culture has to be analyzed.

Exegesis of culture refers to using all of the existing academic disciplines and tools to understand how contemporary culture is seeking to bring meaning to its existence. It is concerned to discover what societal forces are at work that assist or hinder the quest for meaning. The assumption behind the exegesis of culture is that the quest for meaning is basic to human life. After cultural exegesis reveals the various ways culture seeks meaning, the task of the faith community is to be aware of

God's *kairotic* activity and confront the events with the central liberating dynamic of what God is doing.

The Postmodern Age

The quest for meaning takes place within the context of two opposing cultural trends; namely, modernization and countermodernization.[8] Modernization refers to the transformation of the world brought about by industrialization and the technological revolution, and it has had an impact on every dimension of life from the personal to the cultural. Its basic result has been the uprooting of beliefs and values from their traditional moorings, and this has contributed greatly to pluralism and privatism in the religious quest. Moreover, persons have had to pursue ultimate meaning in life without the support of tradition. This has resulted because tradition has been undermined and weakened by technology.

In the midst of modernization, countermodernizing trends have emerged. The critique has come from the academic and the religiously conservative community. From the academic and professional community there are the mental health specialists who have brought attention to the fact that the collapsing of tradition places a real emotional burden on persons. Then, there are those in sociology who emphasize how important small communal groupings are to the transmission of values from one generation to another. They also talk about the importance of small groups for the stability of community. In addition, religious fundamentalism has criticized secularization, the impact of scientific technology, and the rise of impersonal urban civilization.[9] More precisely, the concerns of countermodernizing forces can be summed up in the following: (1) the limitations of scientifically based technological images of human fulfillment, (2) the importance of deep, long-lasting, ongoing personal relationships, (3) the significance of spirituality—the place of transcendence—in secular life, (4) the increased political utility of pushing countermodernizing ideologies, (5) the priority of protesting the greater deterioration of life that results when persons are treated as objects to be exploited, (6) and the importance of forming communal groups where long-lasting relationships can take place.

Harvey Cox in *Religion in the Secular City* has pointed out that the rise to prominence of evangelical conservatives and fundamentalists was not anticipated by the modernists. Moreover, he points out that Latin American liberation theologians share a concern for modernity similar to that of evangelical Christians and fundamentalists. More precisely, Cox has pointed out that the importance of Scripture hermeneutically interpreted within small communally based groups has been the revolutionary element that has given rise to liberation theology and concerns in Latin America.[10]

Of significance in the postmodern age is the emergence of small base communities throughout the world, according to Cox.[11] He points out that there has been an explosion of small face-to-face groups around the world, and these groups include prayer and healing groups, marriage encounter sessions, adult discussions, Bible-study groups, women's and men's fellowships, and consciousness-raising groups. Not all these groups are church related, but they point to an important countermodernizing trend.

For Cox, the base community has three characteristics: (1) a significant degree of lay control and a move toward egalitarianism; (2) an internal liturgical life of singing, praying, and sharing (there is a celebration of the historical images of the biblical faith); and (3) study and critical analysis of the secular situation in the light of the Bible's message that becomes the basis for political engagement.[12] Thus, grassroots religion, or folk religion, is emerging all over the world, and it is the major force in a postmodern age.

Another dimension of postmodernism that is related to a countermodernizing trend is the reconciliation of science and religion. Part of modernism has been the general scientific outlook on the world as self-contained with no supernatural forces intervening or providing direction in any way.[13] However, there is a new rapprochement between science and religion in which the antagonism of the past may be of no lasting significance. Some of the emerging characteristics in the new relationship between science and religion include recognition: (1) that all of reality cannot be understood in naturalistic categories; (2) that the secular view of science has a history dating back to the seventeenth century, but there was a parallel and simultaneous theological view of science which has been ignored[14]; (3) that science progresses through a series of visions or breakthroughs very much akin to insight and revelation in religion[15]; (4) that patterns of energy reflect qualities more akin to the mind or spirit than to tangible physical objects[16]; (5) that matter is dynamic and, therefore, is not a closed system; and (6) that science is beginning to open its door to the miraculous.

The result of these six developments is an increasing openness to the supernatural and the mysterious within culture. Science is no longer going to be dominant outside of a context of values and religion. Thus, the religious quest for meaning can proceed on both religious and secular levels.

Keeping in mind the new rapprochement between science and religion and the critique of modernity by base communities rooted in scriptural study, we reconsider the third step in the hermeneutical process. The ontology of events requires an awareness of God's *kairotic* movement as well as a cultural exegesis. The exegesis or analysis of modernity and postmodernity requires interdisciplinary tools including theological and behavioral science acumen. Thus, the hermeneutics in a postmodern age will draw on interdisciplinary tools, and will be carried out in small face-to-face communities. Bible study, ritual, and the interrelatedness of the community's life will be some of the channels through which God will work to liberate human wholeness. This will be true of black churches as well as white churches.

Of significance is the role of women in the hermeneutical small base community. Their participation was part of the slave tradition, and it will continue in the postmodern period.

Hermeneutical Methods in a Postmodern Age

Hermeneutical methods will reflect methods that were discovered in our study of the slave and ex-slave religious community. Postmodernization can be viewed as a return to premodern forms of community. Thus, the emphasis in postmodernity on face-to-face relationships makes the role of the slave community more valuable for hermeneutics in the contemporary church as a whole.

Perhaps the most significant hermeneutical method emerging out of our study is the hermeneutics of life review. Although the aging person recounts his or her story and reorganizes it in the light of his or her present life, the story itself takes place in a context of interpersonal and intergenerational relationships. The base communities as places of hermeneutical discussion must be intergenerational so that younger generations have the benefit of elders' wisdom in their efforts to bring meaning to their lives. Moreover, the elder will feel affirmed, appreciated, and supported for being permitted to share the life review in community. Hermeneutics, then, has relational and intergenerational dimensions.

The communal-analogy-storytelling-listening model of hermeneutics will also be important in the interpretation and reinterpretation of life. As the small base community engages in Bible study, people will tell their stories and listen to the stories of others in much the same ways as did the slaves and ex-slaves. They will bring their inner experiences (unconscious hermeneutics) and problems of getting along in life into the community, and the result will be a reinterpretation of their situation in life in light of analogous stories in the Bible and the stories of those in the base community. Out of such communal-analogy-storytelling-listening will come holistic growth and the possibility of a holistic response to the liberating activity of God through the service to others.

The cultural hermeneutical method of the slave and ex-slave community is also important. The premodern world view of the slave and ex-slave is not the same world view existing today. Yet, the countermodernizing forces are pointing to the emergence of a premodern world view similar to that of the slaves and ex-slaves—especially in terms of openness to spiritual experiences, the interpenetration of the material and nonmaterial, the corporate nature of life, and proleptic eschatology. The task of cultural hermeneutics within the postmodern age is to recognize how the communal-analogy-storytelling-listening model will help to fashion a new world view similar to but different from the premodern world view of the slave and ex-slave. The task is not to reshape the present in light of the past; rather, the goal is to allow God to work within the ritualistic hermeneutical process in the base community so that meaning for life emerges.

Thus, hermeneutics in postmodern communal settings will not be a return to a premodern world view, but it will be a response to what God is doing through the worship life of the community to bring about a new cultural world view of meaning that is related to the past. The creation of a postmodern world view will grow out of encountering God through Scripture, tradition, ritual, and others in base communities. It will be a response to the storytelling-listening process; it will not be a reactionary desire to return to the past. Dimensions of the past will be embodied in the process of deriving meaning, but the meaning will be vital and new.

Theological Education and Pastoral Counseling Within Hermeneutics

Along with the importance of the small face-to-face groupings in the hermeneutical process within the church, theological education and pastoral counseling are also important settings for hermeneutics. The growing emphasis on small group reflection in field experiences in theological education, on Howard Clinebell's growth counseling model and methods,[17] and the appearance of Charles Gerkin's book *The Living Human Document: Re-Visioning Pastoral Counseling in a Hermeneutical Mode* are evidences of the emerging importance of these two areas. Our concern here is to support the current trends to do hermeneutics in field experiences as well as in pastoral counseling. However, it is also necessary to emphasize that liberal seminaries and pastoral counseling as a movement must recognize that we are in a postmodern period; much of the literature on theological reflection and on pastoral counseling in liberal settings carries many of the assumptions of modernity. Moreover, many theological conservatives go to the other extreme and divorce themselves from any of the behavioral sciences except for cognitive counseling approaches based on biblical principles. Our call is for pastoral counseling and theological education to take seriously the dynamic liberating activity of God to produce human wholeness within the community; to take seriously the role of Scripture and faith heritage in the hermeneutical process; to be open to God's supernatural involvement in life processes as well as God working in naturalistic and incarnational ways; and to assist people who desire to do so to draw on premodern religious images of growth.

The Role of Religious Leaders

Real problems of leadership exist within church groups today which point to the need for democratic, egalitarian, communally based groups. The basis of the leadership problem is that both liberal and conservative churches have bought into bureaucratic organizational styles of rational administration. Harvey Cox calls this organizational style and administration, bureaucratic rationalism; it functions to make transactions smooth and efficient without inviting much intimacy.[18] It is characterized by patterns of domination, control, and top-down administrative procedures. Many conservative leaders use this model of administration to keep their constituents on right countermodernizing trends, while liberal denominations are bogged down trying to make their bureaucracies more democratic. It is very difficult for large bureaucracies to be democratic, and it is difficult for socially charismatic leaders to be democratic. Within small, face-to-face base communities, democracy and egalitarianism are the rule; however, their problem is how these small base communities relate to one another and to the larger groups and organizations of which they are a part.

Our task is not to address the relationship of small, community-based groups to other such groups and to the larger organizations of which they are a part. Rather, we are highlighting the function of the small base community in hermeneutics and the role of the religious leader as facilitating the interpretation and reinterpretation process within the base community. An environment of warmth, caring, and egalitarianism must be created by such a leader. Moreover, the use of ritual, religious songs, and tradition is essential for creating an environment for hermeneutics. Further, the pastor or leader conversant in the different levels of hermeneutics—unconscious hermeneutics, life-review hermeneutics, intergenerational and relational hermeneutics, communal-analogy-story-telling-listening hermeneutics, and communal hermeneutics—enables the community to bring meaning to its life and to its members. Here, then, the style of leadership is facilitating and enabling rather than directive and authoritarian. It is sensitive to God's movement within the community and keeps its members aware of that movement. The authority in that community rests ultimately in God and in the egalitarian relationships.

Case Study

The hermeneutical model fashioned on the thinking of Paul Hanson and reflections on the slave conversion experiences has been introduced in three steps. The case study below will illustrate in detail the major steps of the hermeneutics of engagement. A student presented his dream to members of a personality and religion class at Interdenominational Theological Center. This section picks up the dream material presented in the Preface. The dream had the following content:

I parked my car in a factory parking lot. I got out of the car and went into the factory. There was a conveyor belt where caskets were being moved up to a special room. I found myself on the conveyor belt face down going up to this room. When I arrived at the room a man met me. He said that he was a Jew. This man gave me a ticket receipt, and told me where to go next. I found myself back on the conveyor belt facing up this time on my back. When I got down to the bottom of the conveyor line, I saw a woman who asked me for a ticket, but I had no ticket. I had only the receipt for the ticket. I gave her the receipt, and then I proceeded into a room where the people were gathered in a circle to worship.

128

In helping the person interpret the dream, the class, which was composed of black ministerial students, drew on their own faith heritage—a heritage that was passed on through intergenerational relationships. They concluded that this dream was the dreamer's call to the ministry. To support their conclusion they pointed to the symbolism of the casket which they said symbolized death. They also said that the conveyor belt was a form of unmerited grace which led them to the conclusion that the dream also related to rebirth. The dreamer agreed that this was a special dream and pointed to the Jew who he said represented Jesus Christ. A student remarked, "Yes, Jesus also paid the price for the ticket so that the man could receive salvation."

Up to the introduction of the free-grace theme, symbolized by the ticket receipt, tradition was the dominant interpretive framework. Then the class moved to ask the student dreamer to draw on modern dream theory, especially the theory of Carl Jung, to help understand the psychological and spiritual significance of the dream. It was asserted that in Jungian theory the dream referred to the present state of wholeness of the personality, which was reflected in the death-rebirth theme, and the symbol of wholeness, which is the circle in Jungian theory.

After the student heard the input from the class, he pointed out that his own notions about the experience were confirmed by the class, and he felt affirmed by the class feedback. He also pointed out that he had acted on the dream by giving up his job in order to enter seminary. He said that the dream was his call to ministry, and the dream was the beginning of a second career.

Discernment of God's Activity

The interpreters of the dream, including the dreamer, were aware of the liberating activity of God in the Scriptures and in the black Christian tradition. The themes interpreted in the dream—the call, unmerited grace, and the payment of Jesus for atonement—were all dimensions of the liberating act of God in Scripture and tradition. These students drew on their knowledge about the person and their knowledge of the work of Jesus the liberator gleaned from their own experience, their faith tradition, and study of Scripture to interpret the religious experience of the individual. Since this interpretation took place within a theological setting, it can be assumed that critical reflective abilities were operative. The students were mostly third year seminarians who were concerned to correlate what they learned in their studies with their own experiences and the practice of ministry.

These students also were keenly oriented to the experiential catching of God's movement in their heritage. They came as full participants in their own faith heritage in which they encountered the liberating activity of God. Their existential experience of God, buttressed by technical reason, gave them a frame of reference that they brought to bear on the dreamer's experience. They transferred knowledge from their encounters with God and their studies into another context. They were able to transfer their own understanding of how God met their needs to similar needs of another person. Indeed, it was their faith heritage and God's working in it that enabled them to help the student dreamer to interpret his dream.

Participation in God's Liberating Activity in Community

It is often quite difficult to conceive of a theological seminary as an extension of the church's ministry. Traditional loyalties to the university and diversity of orientation from professor to professor contribute to the difficulty of defining the ministry of the theological seminary. However, greater clarity among faculties regarding their mission to students is emerging as faculty and students engage in reflection on the practice of ministry and the emotional, spiritual, and professional growth needs of students. Increasingly, then, seminaries are expecting students to move dialogically from the faith heritage to the practice of ministry. The professional, intellectual, spiritual, and emotional development of students is indeed an extension of the ministry known as the equipping of the saints.

Within the purpose of theological education to equip students for ministry is the specific intent of each course. The specific intent of the personality and religion course was to help the student become aware of the role of personality theory in understanding the factors that aid or hinder growth toward wholeness. A related goal of the course was for the student to relate theology and psychology to his or her own life in ways that provided the possibility of further growth. A final goal of the course was to enable students to become committed to their own growth and to the growth of others.

The case study demonstrated that the last goal, becoming committed to one's own growth and the growth of others, was being actualized. The student dreamer sought feedback from his peers so that he could make a better commitment to his call. The other students gladly participated. This added to their commitment to another person. The student dreamer also participated in giving feedback to others, thus making mutual commitment a reality.

Being committed to the growth of another is an extension of the liberating activity of God. Participating in a course which focuses on the human growth process also relates to being related to God's liberating activity. Moreover, God's liberating activity was operative in this class through the feedback process. In a very meaningful way the structure of the class, the actual execution of its goals, and student involvement represented the second step of the hermeneutical model; this step is the commitment by people within the faith community to the central dynamic activity of God. A seminary classroom qualifies as an arena where God's liberating activity to help students grow holistically is at work. In fact, God's liberating activity can work holistically throughout the entire seminary curriculum, and this would lead to interdisciplinary, integrated theological education for growth and service.

Fidelity to the Ontology of Events

The third step in the hermeneutics of engagement brings God's liberating acts to bear upon contemporary events within the faith community. The contemporary event in this case was the dream of the seminary student. It was God at work in the inner life of the student that needed to be addressed.

Often students are reluctant to communicate such experiences in an academic setting for fear of being labeled as strange. Yet, students often are eager to share such experiences when there is openness and sensitivity to such experiences. Communicating such experiences will become more commonplace when seminaries become more sensitive to the postmodern trends being actualized in the experiences of students.

Part of the ontology of events in hermeneutics is the use of contemporary behavioral science tools to exegete culture. In the specific case, the exegesis was not of culture, but of a person. Carl Jung's psychology was drawn on because it examines some of the theological images reported in the dream. Thus, psychological, biblical, and theological images entered into the hermeneutical dialogue. Thus, the student was not confined to biblical or theological images, but analogous psychological images were drawn on to produce meaning. Theology and psychology, via the vehicle of similarity in images, became hermeneutical tools for understanding God's liberation of human growth.

Another important dimension of the third hermeneutical step is the context in which the hermeneutical process occurred. It occurred in a class with about seventeen students. This could qualify as a small base community in that the atmosphere was created for sharing, support, and growth. According to our study and the postmodern age's emphasis on small face-to-face communities, this seminary classroom was an ideal place for hermeneutics.

The hermeneutics processes involved in the case study were relational and communal and used the hermeneutical method of analogy-storytelling-listening. The expectation of the course was that students would relate to one another supportively and would share their own stories. By way of analogy in shared stories, they helped others to interpret and reinterpret their stories. The student in the case shared his story; and while others did not share their stories at that point, they did respond to the dreamer out of their own stories.

The role of the leader or the teacher was to create an environment of trust, care, and support. Although there are some administrative nonegalitarian aspects to a student-teacher relationship, a caring, facilitative environment can be established. The case study demonstrated that it is possible to create a caring environment for hermeneutics.

Postscript

Our task in this chapter has been to draw implications of the study of the slave and ex-slave conversion tradition for a model of hermeneutics that could be relevant to the church in general. This model was presented and illustrated by a brief case study. While the model came out of the correlation of the black tradition with a model of hermeneutics in an academic setting, it does have practical implications for ministry in broad terms.

Significant in postmodern trends will be the place of feminine theology in hermeneutics. Black women were prominent in the development of the hermeneutical process in the slave and ex-slave community, and their contribution was explored. Egalitarianism within small base communities will further assist women to be involved in the new reversal in theology where the last become first and the first become team members. Indeed, the future of hermeneutics and its importance for community will occur in small face-to-face communities. Women will play a major role in these hermeneutical groups.

Notes

1. Paul Tillich, *Theology of Culture* (New York: Oxford University Press, 1964), p. 45.
2. Harvey Cox, *Religion in the Secular City: Toward a Postmodern Theology* (New York: Simon & Schuster, 1984), p. 43.
3. Tillich, *Theology of Culture*, p. 45.
4. Ibid., pp. 45-49.
5. Cox, *Religion in the Secular City*, pp. 175-80.

6. Paul Hanson, *Dynamic Transcendence* (Philadelphia: Fortress Press, 1978), pp. 61-90.

7. Tillich, *Theology of Culture*, p. 20.

8. Peter Berger, *Facing Up to Modernity* (New York: Harper & Row, Basic Books, 1977), pp. 70-80.

9. Cox, *Religion in the Secular City*, pp. 39-48.

10. Ibid., pp. 85-90.

11. Ibid., pp. 107-17.

12. Ibid., p. 108.

13. Yandall Woodfin, *With All Your Mind: A Christian Philosophy* (Nashville: Abingdon Press, 1980), p. 173.

14. David Griffin, "Theology and the Rise of Modern Science," unpublished article, School of Theology at Claremont, Calif., November 1982.

15. Woodfin, *With All Your Heart*, p. 185.

16. Ibid., p. 189.

17. Howard Clinebell, *Basic Types of Pastoral Care and Counseling* (Nashville: Abingdon Press, 1984).

18. Cox, *Religion in the Secular City*, pp. 183-90.

BIBLIOGRAPHICAL
SOURCES: SLAVE MATERIAL

Allen, Richard. *The Life Experience and Gospel Labors of the Rt. Rev. Richard Allen.* Nashville: Abingdon Press, 1983.

Bayliss, John, ed. *Black Slave Narratives.* New York: Macmillan, 1970.

Bernard, Jacqueline. *Journey Toward Freedom. The Story of Sojourner Truth.* New York: W. W. Norton & Co., 1967.

Botkin, Benjamin A., ed. *Lay My Burden Down: A Folk History of Slavery.* Chicago: University of Chicago Press, 1958.

Bradford, Sarah H. *Harriet: The Moses of Her People.* New York: Lockwood & Son, 1886. Reprint. New York: Corinth Books, 1961.

Brewer, J. Mason, ed. *American Negro Folklore.* Chicago: Times Books, 1968.

Cone, Cecil. *The Identity Crisis in Black Theology.* Nashville: AMEC Press, 1975.

Courlander, Harold. *Negro Folk Music, U.S.A.* New York: Columbia University Press, 1963.

Craft, William and Craft, Ellen. *Running a Thousand Miles for Freedom: Or, the Escape of William and Ellen Craft from Slavery.* London: Tweedie, 1860. Reprint. The American Negro: His History and Literature, Ser. 3, edited by William L. Katz, New York: Arno Press, 1970.

Douglass, Frederick. *Narrative of the Life of Frederick Douglass, an American Slave,* written by himself. 1845. Reprint, Benjamin Quales, ed. Cambridge, Mass.: Harvard University Press, Belknap Press, 1960.

Dubois, W. E. B. *The Souls of Black Folk: Essays and Sketches.* Greenwich, Conn.: Fawcett Publications, 1961. Millwood, N.Y.: Kraus-Thomson Organization, Kraus Reprint, 1973.

Genovese, Eugene D. *Roll, Jordan Roll: The World the Slaves Made.* New York: Random House, Vintage Books, 1972; Pantheon Books, 1974.

Gutman, Herbert G. *The Black Family in Slavery and Freedom 1750–1925.* New York: Random House, Vintage Books, 1979.

Hairston, Jester. "Elijah Rock." Choral arrangement. Bourne Publishing Co., 1965.

Haskins, James S. *Witchcraft, Mysticism and Magic in the Black World.* Garden City, N.Y.: Doubleday, 1974.

Herskovits, Melville J. *The Myth of the Negro Past.* 1958. Reprint. Gloucester, Mass.: Peter Smith, 1970.

Hughes, Langston, and Bontemps, Arna, eds. *The Book of Negro Folklore.* New York: Dodd, Mead & Co., 1959.

Hughes, Louis. *Thirty Years a Slave: From Bondage to Freedom.* Milwaukee: South Side Printing Co., 1897. Reprint. Westport Conn.: Greenwood Press, Negro University Press, 1969.

Johnson, Clifton H., ed. *God Struck Me Dead: Religious Conversion Experiences of Ex-slaves.* Philadelphia: Pilgrim Press, 1969.

Johnson, J. R., and J. W. Johnson. *The Books of American Negro Spirituals.* New York: Viking Press, 1964.

Jones, Charles C., Jr. *Negro Myths from the Georgia Coast: Told in the Vernacular.* Boston: Hougton, Mifflin & Co., 1888. Reprint. Detroit-Gale Research Co., 1969.

Katz, William L., ed. *The American Negro: His History and Literature.* New York: Arno Press and the New York Times, Ser. 1, 44 books, 1968; Ser. 2, 66 books, 1969; Ser. 3, 30 books, 1970.

Lane, Lunsford. *The Narrative of Lunsford Lane.* The American Negro: His History and Literature, Ser. 1.

Levine, Lawrence J. *Black Culture and Black Consciousness: Afro-American Folk Thought from Slavery to Freedom.* New York: Oxford University Press, 1977.

Lovell, John. *Black Songs: The Forge and the Flame.* New York: Macmillan Co., 1972.

Mays, Benjamin E. *The Negro's God as Reflected in His Literature.* New York: Antheneum, Chapman and Grimes, 1938. Reprint. New York: Antheneum Publishers, 1968.

Mbiti, John S. *African Religions and Philosophy.* Garden City, N.Y.: Doubleday, 1970.

———. *New Testament Eschatology in an African Background.* London: Oxford University Press, 1971.

Mitchell, Henry H. *Black Belief: Folk Beliefs of Blacks in America and West Africa.* New York: Harper & Row, Publishers, 1975.

———. "The Black Religious Tradition." Th.D. diss., School of Theology at Claremont, 1973.

Nichols, Charles H. *Many Thousand Gone: The Ex-slaves Account of Their Bondage and Freedom.* Bloomington: Indiana University Press, 1963 (Reprint. Harcourt, Brace & World, 1965.)

Osofsky, Gilbert, ed. *Puttin' on Ole Massa: The Slave Narratives of*

Henry Bibb, William W. Brown, and Solomon Northrup. New York: Harper & Row, Publishers, 1969.

Pennington, James W. C. *The Fugitive Blacksmith.* London: Charles Gilpin, 1849. Reprint, *The American Negro: His History and Literature,* edited by William L. Katz.

Puckett, Newbell, *Folk Beliefs of the Southern Negro.* Chapel Hill: University of North Carolina Press, 1926.

Raboteau, Albert J. *Slave Religion: The "Invisible Institution" in the Antebellum South.* New York: Oxford University Press, 1978.

Rawich, George P., ed. *The American Slave: A Composite Autobiography.* 19 vols. Contributions in Afro-American and African Studies, no. 11. Westport, Conn.: Greenwood Press, 1972.

———. *The American Slave: A Composite Autobiography.* vol. 18, *Unwritten History of Slavery.* Westport, Conn.: Greenwood Press, 1972.

Songs of Zion. Supplemental Worship Resources 12. Nashville: Abingdon Press, 1981.

Steward, Austin. *Twenty-Two Years a Slave and Forty Years a Freeman.* 1856. Reprint. Westport, Conn.: Greenwood Press, Negro University Press, 1968.

Stroyer, Jacob. *My Life in the South.* Salem, Mass.: Newcomb and Gauss, 1898. Reprint, *The American Negro: His History and Literature,* Ser. 1, edited by William L. Katz.

Thompson, George, *Prison Life and Reflections: A Narrative.* Hartford: A Work, 1849.

Thompson, John. *Life of John Thompson, a Fugitive Slave.* 1856. Reprint. Westport, Conn.: Greenwood Press, Negro University Press, 1968.

Thurman, Howard. *Deep River: Reflections on the Religious Insight of Certain of the Negro Spirituals.* New York: Harper and Bro., 1955.

———. *The Negro Spiritual Speaks of Life and Death.* New York: Harper and Bro., 1947.

———. *With Head and Heart: The Autobiography.* New York: Harcourt Brace Jovanovich, 1979.

Truth, Sojourner. *Narrative of Sojourner Truth.* Boston: J. B. Yerrington and Son, 1850.

Washington, Booker T. *Up from Slavery.* Garden City, N.Y.: Doubleday, 1963.

Wilmore, Gayraud S. *Last Things First.* Philadelphia: The Westminster Press, 1982.

Wink, Robin et al. "An Autobiography of the Reverend Josiah Henson," in *Four Fugitive Slave Narratives.* Reading, Mass.: Addison-Wesley Publishing Co., 1969.

INDEX